# REST

# REST

Experiencing God's Peace
in a Restless World

Siang-Yang Tan, Ph.D.

REGENT COLLEGE PUBLISHING
Vancouver, British Columbia

First published 2000 by Vine Books, an imprint of Servant Publications.

This edition published 2003 by
Regent College Publishing
5800 University Boulevard
Vancouver, B.C. V6T 2E4 Canada
<www.regentpublishing.com>

Views and opinions expressed in works published by Regent College
Publishing are those of the authors and may not necessarily represent the
official position of Regent College <www.regent-college.edu>.

Cover image copyright © 2003 by Regent College and its licensors.

National Library of Canada Cataloguing in Publication Data

Tan, Siang-Yang
  Rest: experiencing God's peace in a restless world / Siang-Yang Tan.

Includes bibliographical references and index.
ISBN 1-57383-274-X

  1. Rest—Religious aspects—Christianity. 2. Christian life. I. Title.

BV4597.55.T36 2003      248.4          C2003-905300-8

The Rev. Siang-Yang Tan, Ph.D. (McGill University), is senior pastor of First Evangelical Church Glendale and Professor of Psychology at Fuller Theological Seminary in Pasadena, California. He is a licensed psychologist and has written several books, including *Lay Counseling* (Zondervan, 1991), *Managing Chronic Pain* (InterVarsity, 1996), *Coping With Depression* (Baker, 1995, with Dr. John Ortberg), and *Disciplines of the Holy Spirit* (Zondervan, 1997, with Dr. Douglas Gregg).

To Angela

With all my love, gratitude, support, and prayers.

# CONTENTS

# FOREWORD

Several years ago, some of the students I knew at Fuller Seminary affectionately referred to their professor, Siang-Yang Tan, as the "Orient Express." Like that famous train, he moved from place to place with efficiency and great speed, always on the go, constantly pushing himself and others to meet schedules and keep moving forward. At the time I admired his drive and productivity, maybe in part because I was the same.

I'm making progress but I still struggle with a breathless lifestyle. I suspect Dr. Tan is the same. Yet over the years I have seen a different side of my friend emerge. It is a side that is less driven, more sensitive, incredibly supportive, and growing in spiritual depth. He still is productive as a pastor, psychologist, public speaker, and professor, but he radiates a deepening love for Christ and a passion to guide others as they grow in Christ-likeness.

In this book, Siang-Yang Tan draws from a richness of experience and knowledge to write with warmth and compassion. Since he knows the difficulty of slowing down in these hyperactive times, he is able to give practical guidelines to others, drawn from a wealth of information found in the Scriptures, empirical research, and psychological reports. His book taps into the wisdom of numerous writers in fields as diverse as theology, spiritual formation, psychology, and physiology. And in it all, he writes with clarity and contemporary relevance.

An Orient Express could not have stopped long enough to write a book like this. It only could have been produced by a brother who has learned to slow down, rest in the Lord, and wait patiently for Him.

If rest is not high on your agenda or not easy to put into practice, learn from an author who is growing at a healthy pace and willing to bring others along on the journey. You will be glad you stepped on board.

Gary R. Collins, Ph.D.

# ACKNOWLEDGMENTS

First of all, I would like to thank Gwen Ellis, former senior acquisitions editor, and Bert Ghezzi, vice president and editorial director of Servant Publications, for inviting me to write this book on rest. I would also like to thank Kathryn Deering, senior editor, and Helen Motter for their helpful editorial feedback and revisions. It was a joy working with them and the rest of the Servant Publications staff.

Special thanks to Dr. Gary Collins, who is a dear friend and brother in Christ, for kindly writing the foreword. I deeply appreciate him and his writings. I am also grateful for special friends on the RENOVARE Board, including Dr. Richard Foster and Dr. Dallas Willard, for their spiritually renewing fellowship, support, and prayers. The prayer support of many intercessors, especially from my church, First Evangelical Church Glendale, is greatly appreciated.

I want to thank Fuller Theological Seminary for granting me a sabbatical in the fall of 1999, during which most of this book was written. The excellent secretarial help of Judith Griesinger at Fuller is also gratefully acknowledged, as is the extra typing done by Matt Westbrook.

The constant and consistent love, support, and prayers of Angela, my wife, and Carolyn and Andrew, our teenage children, helped me to complete writing this book. They are among God's greatest blessings in my life, and I deeply love and appreciate them.

Most of all, I want to thank God—Father, Son, and Holy Spirit—for guiding me as I wrote and for letting me experience more deeply the rest of His grace and the grace of His rest.

Siang-Yang Tan
Arcadia, California

# INTRODUCTION

As I write this introduction, I have literally dozens of books and articles before me that touch on the deep longings of our hearts for *rest*—for quiet, peace, contentment, refreshment, stillness, tranquility, homeostasis, being collected, calm, centered, renewed. Among the titles of books that have been published recently are (in alphabetical order of authors' names): *Breathless: Transform Your Time-Starved Days into A LIFE WELL LIVED*, by Gary R. Collins (Wheaton, Ill.: Tyndale, 1998); *Keeping the Sabbath Wholly: Ceasing, Resting, Embracing, Feasting*, by Marva J. Dawn (Grand Rapids, Mich.: Eerdmans, 1989); *Keep a Quiet Heart*, by Elisabeth Elliot (Ann Arbor, Mich.: Servant/Vine, 1995); *Finding Serenity in the Age of Anxiety*, by Robert Gerzon (New York: Macmillan, 1997); *The Anxiety Cure: You Can Find Emotional Tranquillity and Wholeness*, by Archibald D. Hart (Nashville: Word, 1999); *Stopping: How to Be Still When You Have to Keep Going*, by David Kundtz (New York: MJF, 1998); *Be Still My Soul: Resting in the Greatness of God and His Love for You*, by Martyn Lloyd-Jones (Ann Arbor, Mich.: Servant/Vine, 1995); *Sabbath: Restoring the Sacred Rhythm of Rest*, by Wayne Muller (New York: Bantam, 1999); *Right-Sizing Your Life: The Up Side of Slowing Down*, by Philip D. Patterson and Michael W. Herndon (Downers Grove, Ill.: InterVarsity Press, 1998); *Margin: Restoring Emotional, Physical, Financial, and Time Reserves to Overloaded Lives*, by Richard A. Swenson (Colorado Springs, Colo.: NavPress, 1992); *The Overload Syndrome:*

*Learning to Live Within Your Limits,* by Richard A. Swenson (Colorado Springs, Colo.: NavPress, 1998); *Finding Contentment: When Momentary Happiness Just Isn't Enough,* by Neil Clark Warren (Nashville: Nelson, 1997); and *Simplify Your Life and Get More Out of It!,* by H. Norman Wright (Wheaton, Ill.: Tyndale, 1998). There are other titles I have not mentioned. It's tiring just reading this list!

There is no doubt at all that we are living in an age of anxiety and deep restlessness, with inner and outer turmoil. Anxiety has become the number one emotional problem today, closely tied to depression. Many people ache for rest and peace. In fact, experiencing rest is so difficult for most people that a magazine called *The Life@Work Journal,* which seeks to blend biblical wisdom and business excellence, recently dedicated a whole issue (July/August 1999, Vol. 2, No. 4) to "The Hard Work of Rest"!

This book on rest deals with the topic head-on. In Part I, "Explaining Rest," we will look at the contrast between rest and unrest and the main characteristics of rest—physical, emotional, relational, and spiritual.

Part II gets to the meat of the book: experiencing rest. From a biblical perspective, we will discuss various ways of entering into the rest we all so deeply desire: Shepherd-centeredness in Christ, Spirit-filled surrender, solitude and silence, simplicity, sabbath, sleep, spiritual community, servanthood, and stress management. Finally, in Part III, we will look at eternal rest, with overwhelming gratitude for rest assured because of the Gospel of salvation through Jesus Christ. He loved us and gave Himself for us so that we may live forever and rest forever in and through Him!

May God, the Author of true and eternal rest and peace, grant you deep experiences of His rest as you read this book and apply it to your life!

The Lord bless you and keep you; the Lord make his face shine upon you and be gracious to you; the Lord turn his face toward you and give you peace.

NUMBERS 6:24-26

Come to me, all you who are weary and burdened, and I will give you rest. Take my yoke upon you and learn from me, for I am gentle and humble in heart, and you will find rest for your souls. For my yoke is easy and my burden is light.

MATTHEW 11:28-30

*Part One:*

# Explaining
# Rest

*One*

~

# Rest and Unrest

When I first mentioned to people that I was writing a book on rest, their primary response was an overwhelmingly positive one, indicating great interest in the topic. Most of them said they could not wait to read the book. Many commented on how busy and stressed out they were, expressing a deep desire for rest.

We all realize that we are truly living in an age of anxiety. Anxiety has become the leading emotional problem of our day.[1] When I ask people, "How are you doing?" the most common replies include "I'm really busy." "I'm exhausted! There's just too much to do!" "I'm tired. I need a vacation!" "I'm burned out. There's too much going on." And "I'm so stressed out. I can't keep up anymore!"

As author and physician Richard Swenson has written, the buzzwords of our lives today are: Busyness. Stress. Overload. The demands of life have far outgrown the resources we have to meet them, leading to what he has termed "The Overload Syndrome." Swenson writes, "People are exhausted.... People are stressed.... People are overloaded.... We need more time. We need more space. We need more reserves. We need more buffer."[2]

In a recent interview with Kirk Livingston in *The Life@Work Journal,* Swenson explained a new concept:

> [It's] the body's condition when it is "tightly wound." I call it "torque," and it has to do with the tightness of our muscles and vigilance of our psyche. Healthy rest comes when we allow our high degree of torque completely to unwind. But when torque is at too high a level, it requires an extended period to come down to a restful baseline. Torque isn't easily switched off like a light switch. It only backs off slowly. Many people are wound so tightly they can take months or even years to unwind.... The stressful and overloaded conditions of our world keep most of us in such a high state of torque that we seldom experience true rest.[3]

With such overload and torque in many of our lives, it is no wonder that rest is so difficult to find and the longing for rest is greater than ever. The statistics show that the average American worker actually has added about a month to the work year in the past twenty years. Women today work (at paid jobs) an average of 41.7 hours and men 48.8 hours a week. It was predicted in the 1960s that by 1990 people would be working an average of 20 hours a week and have more leisure time. This prediction has not come true!

Closely related to overwork and overload is our preoccupation with speed. Technological advances in this computer age have left many of us breathless and worn out. In our embrace of speed, we are obsessed with efficiency and productivity. We are horrified at the thought of wasting any time. Bill Gates recently wrote a book entitled *Business at the Speed of Thought.*[4] James Gleick's latest book captures the spirit of our hurried and harried age even more accurately: *Faster: The Acceleration of Just About Everything*.[5] In trying to beat the clock, we walk faster, drive faster, work faster. But at a great cost. Levels of stress and anxiety are increased exponentially. *Unrest* is the result. Unrest is feeling fearful, anxious, panicked, scattered, harried, hurried, overwhelmed, exhausted, discontent, driven, stressed. It's the opposite of what we most deeply long for: rest.

People are seeking rest today with a vengeance! They are taking stress-management classes, learning to meditate, doing yoga, going on retreats, getting into spirituality of all kinds (including New Age versions, Eastern mysticism, and Buddhism), and trying hard to change their lifestyles so they can find some peace and rest again. Ironically, more and more people are stressed out trying to overcome stress. We try too hard to find rest, and the hard work of rest often leads to further unrest and restlessness. We need to have a deeper, more biblical understanding of rest and how to experience or enter into rest—God's rest, in God's way.

## Defining Rest

*Rest* can be described as a state of peace, contentment, serenity, refreshment, stillness, tranquility, or calm. The qualities of rest include:

- quietness of heart
- a sober awareness of who we are and who God is
- an ability to let go (and *not* try so hard, even at resting!)
- an ability to enjoy leisure, nature, and things that do not involve performance
- reflection

- trust
- an ability to live from our higher or true self—to determine our values and live by them; enjoying the moment—not living in the past or the future
- "breathing easy" (and deeply!)
- waiting without impatience
- not being impulsive or rash

Whole books could be—and have been—written about many of these aspects of rest.

Gordon MacDonald has rightly differentiated rest from leisure or mere amusement; he tells us that rest is found beyond leisure. It is God who instituted and commanded rest—true Sabbath rest—for humankind (see Ex 20:8-11; 34:21). He is also the first "rester" Himself (see Gn 2:2-3; Ex 31:17). MacDonald points out:

> This rest was not meant to be a luxury, but rather a *necessity* for those who want to have growth and maturity. Since we have not understood that rest is a necessity, we have perverted its meaning, substituting for the rest that God first demonstrated things called leisure or amusement…. Leisure and amusement may be enjoyable, but they are to the private world of the individual like cotton candy to the digestive system. They provide a momentary lift, but they will not last…. The world and the church need genuinely *rested* Christians: Christians who are regularly refreshed by true Sabbath rest, not just leisure or time off. When a godly rest is achieved, you will see just how tough and resilient Christians can actually be.[6]

In *The Life@Work Journal*, Thomas Addington and Stephen Graves have noted that three main words are used in the Old Testament to describe rest: *Sabat*, the Hebrew word for Sabbath, meaning to stop or cease from work and activity; *Nuah*, meaning to settle down with no more movement but with a sense of inner ease or security; and *Saqat*, meaning tranquility and absence of inner anxiety and external pressure. Addington and Graves conclude:

> Taken together, the three terms paint us a rich and multi-faceted picture. Rest involves something we do, something we experience and something God gives us. We see that we must regularly cease from our work and become still before God to gain a sense of tranquility and to loose the shackles of stress. God provides supernatural security and peace.[7]

Addington and Graves also helpfully point out that we should not think of work *versus* rest but work *and* rest. "God invented both at virtually the same time; they are meant to complement, not fight against each other.... A godly life is a life of rest. A godly life is a life of work. Scripture places rest and work side by side and sees them both as good."[8]

## Our Fear of Rest

Despite our deep desire to experience true Sabbath rest, many of us, ironically, are actually afraid of rest. Why do we fear the very rest that we long for?

There may be various reasons. First, we may be addicted to the adrenaline rush of busyness. In our fast-paced world many of us try to fill every minute with activity of some sort. Archibald Hart has written a whole book on adrenaline and stress, emphasizing how harmful such adrenaline addiction ultimately is to our body, mind, and spirit.[9]

Second, we may be afraid of rest because we are fearful of facing our true state of being: our emptiness, our bad feelings, our painful memories. It is easier and more comfortable to keep busy, to keep going on without stopping to rest. Resting and reflecting may bring us face to face with painful inner feelings and struggles we would rather avoid or keep out of our consciousness.

Third, we may be fearful of rest because we tend to define ourselves by what we produce or how we perform. We have a tendency to use external criteria of success to define our self-worth. Many of us feel we must continue to produce, perform, excel, keep up. We are afraid to slow down and rest because we may be left behind in our business or careers. Promotions may be so important to our self-worth that we dare not slow down or stop to rest, even periodically, for fear that our productivity may drop.

Fourth, closely connected to the previous reason, many of us may feel that it's all up to us to "make it" in life, believing that if we slow down or change, things will simply fall apart. It's not just a matter of keeping up with the Joneses, it is keeping up with the accelerated pace of life in the twenty-first century! "Efficiency" is today's business buzzword. If we don't do business at the speed of thought, fully using the latest computer technology, we may be doomed to failure. Many of us are afraid of rest because we are afraid of losing speed, losing ground, and losing our lifestyles.

Finally, we may be afraid of rest because we feel trapped in our ever-increasing cycle of activity and accelerated busyness. We can't see a way out. The situation may appear so hopeless and helpless that we give up trying to rest at all. In fact, to stop and rest makes us feel more anxious about all the things we are leaving undone. We end up avoiding rest and trying to do even more in the time-starved days of our lives.

## Avoiding Rest

We continue to suffer from the disease of "hurry sickness." John Ortberg has wisely written, "Hurry is the great enemy of spiritual life in our day. Hurry can destroy our souls. Hurry can keep us from living well." Ortberg quotes Carl Jung: "Hurry is not of the devil; hurry *is* the devil."[10] The enemy of our souls knows full well how hurry sickness or unrest can ultimately destroy us. He will do his best to keep us from God's rest. He entices us to drive ourselves onward, create ever more activity, fill our emptiness with external stimuli to avoid the disquiet in our soul. Consequently, we often clutch at people, things, and activities that keep us engaged in the cycle of a hurried and harried life.

## Eliminating Hurry and Finding Rest

John Ortberg is now a teaching pastor at Willow Creek Community Church in South Barrington, Illinois, working and ministering closely with Bill Hybels, the senior pastor. When John first moved from California to Chicago to join Bill's pastoral team, he called his spiritual mentor for some words of wisdom. He had a specific question: "What do I need to do to be spiritually healthy?" After a long pause, his wise spiritual mentor replied, *"You must ruthlessly eliminate hurry from your life."*

John took note of this on paper. Then he asked his mentor, "Now, what else is there?"

After another long pause, the man replied, "There is nothing else. You must ruthlessly eliminate hurry from your life."[11]

Let us explore together how to eliminate hurry from our lives and how to enter instead into God's rest. Despite our mixed feelings about rest—both wanting and yet avoiding it—we know deep inside that we really do desire true Sabbath rest. God put that longing in our hearts when He created us. That longing is ultimately for God Himself, the source of all true rest: physical, emotional, relational, and spiritual. The next chapter will describe these major types of rest more fully.

*Two*

∾

# Rest:
# Physical, Emotional,
# Relational, Spiritual

The patients who come to my office do not seem rested. For that matter, neither do most physicians. The medical residents I teach often are five minutes away from collapse. Many people I meet look haggard and worn out.... We are a tired generation, one for which Matthew Arnold's "hurry sickness" has become a way of life. Our carburetors are set on high, and our gears are stuck in overdrive. Our lives are nonstop.... We have leisure but little rest.[1]

These insightful words from Swenson describe well the physical, emotional, relational, and spiritual states of unrest, fatigue, and "torque" that most of us experience in our world today. Swenson emphasizes that most of us in our daily lives need rest in at least three areas: *physical rest,* which he believes is the least important; *emotional rest,* which is more important by several degrees of magnitude; and *spiritual rest,*which is of the greatest importance, though it is neglected by many.[2]

In this chapter, I will expand upon these aspects of rest and add one more, what I call *relational* rest.

*Physically,* many of us suffer today from heart disease as well as other stress-related illnesses, including addictions, panic attacks, exhaustion, insomnia, headaches, muscle tension, and high blood pressure. Such physical suffering often stems from our inability to manage our lives and to learn how to rest.

*Emotionally,* many of us feel as if we can't keep up with the demands and stresses of our lives. The results often include depression, anxiety, panic, fear, confusion, and feeling trapped or overwhelmed. Our overstimulated emotions need a rest!

*Relationally,* many of us experience what Swenson has called "restless relationships" or "fractured relationships."[3] Whether in the home, church, school, workplace, or the larger community of which we are a part, the presence of unresolved conflicts, broken relationships, misunderstandings, contention, bitterness, strife, and especially an unforgiving spirit can cause much unrest and pain. It is easy to see that relational rest is really another aspect of emotional rest.

*Spiritually,* many of us find it difficult to trust God, to hear His voice, to sense His presence. God seems far away, and the weight of the world rests on our shoulders. We may have an exaggerated sense of self, leading us to believe it is up to us alone to free ourselves from this burden. We may go through the motions of trusting in God but do not reap the rewards or blessings. We search for new techniques in the hope of finding some rest, spiritual serenity, or peace.

Let's look more closely at each kind of rest.

## Physical Rest

Although physical rest may not be the most important aspect of rest we need, it is still an essential type of rest for which our tired bodies yearn. The frenzied activity of our overly busy schedules day in and day out leaves most of us physically drained and fatigued. In a culture that idolizes productivity, work dominates our lives and squeezes out other crucial needs, such as rest and play. Even when we play, we tend to play as hard as we work, if not harder, bringing about greater fatigue instead of rest!

Physical rest includes time for leisure and sleep, especially taking a Sabbath day off each week and sleeping at least eight hours a night. It also involves good nutrition, regular exercise, and practicing at least one good relaxation technique as part of stress management. We protect our physical rest by refusing to overwork and making sure we have enough of a time buffer. Specific strategies for physical rest will be described in more detail in subsequent chapters.

## Emotional Rest

Emotional rest means experiencing peace, quiet, tranquility, contentment, serenity, and refreshment instead of anxiety, fear, panic, tension, discontent, depression, exhaustion, and fatigue. Intellectual or mental rest is part of emotional rest. If our minds are at rest, our emotions can relax. Emotional rest also comes from spiritual rest. Much of this book is devoted to the spiritual aspects of rest because, ultimately, all the dimensions of rest are interconnected and integrated within our human spirits.

## Relational Rest

Relational rest, which is our experience of peace and harmony in our relationships with people, is another type of rest we all desire. In our homes, churches, schools, workplaces, and the larger community in which we live, relational rest can be found in the context of our caring and loving relationships with other people. Such relationships don't work without a heart of love and a soul that is experiencing some level of spiritual and emotional peace deep within. Our spiritual, emotional, and physical rest are all deepened when we receive the gifts of loving and caring relationships in a community of people who believe in Jesus Christ, who are members of His body, the church. It works both ways: relational rest contributes depth and balance to community life, while at the same time requiring true community for its existence.

We all need fellowship and deep friendships that are steeped in prayer and filled with open sharing and forgiveness. Several Christian authors, such as Larry Crabb, Marva Dawn, Stanley Grenz, and Rod Wilson, have recently written very helpful books touching on the theme of Christian community and its relevance to relational rest and wholeness.[4] Their work will be included in the chapter on spiritual community.

## Spiritual Rest

This is by far the most crucial type of rest, although many of us miss it. We all long for spiritual rest in the deepest part of our beings. We need rest from our guilt, doubt, confusion, emptiness, dryness, and despair. We long for the peace of God that transcends all understanding (see Phil 4:7). Such supernatural peace comes when we learn to pray with thanksgiving (see Phil 4:6) and to cast all our cares or anxiety upon Him because He cares for us (see 1 Pt 5:7).

The writer of the book of Hebrews specifically deals with spiritual rest—God's rest—in Hebrews 4:1: "Therefore, since the promise of entering his rest still stands, let us be careful that none of you be found to have fallen short of it." The promise of entering into or experiencing God's rest—true spiritual rest in Him—is still true for the people of God. God's rest is available today to those of us who believe in the gospel of Jesus Christ and receive His rest by faith (Heb 4:2-3). Such spiritual rest from God includes a Sabbath rest (Heb 4:9) in which we rest from our own work just as God did from His (Heb 4:10). Ultimately, of course, God's perfect Sabbath rest can only be fully experienced in heaven to come. However, we can still enter into His rest experientially now by maintaining an active faith relationship with the One who invented rest in the first place.

F.B. Meyer called the theme in Hebrews 4 the Gospel of Rest or the good news of rest. He wrote:

> When we once learn to live by faith, believing that our Father loves us, and will not forget or forsake us, but is pledged to supply all our needs; when we acquire the holy habit of talking to Him about all, and handing all over to Him, at the moment that the tiniest shadow is cast upon the soul; when we accept insult, and annoyance, and interruption, coming to us from whatever quarter as being His permission, and therefore, as part of His dear will for us—then we have learnt the secret of the Gospel of Rest.[5]

Louis Evans, senior pastor of the National Presbyterian Church in Washington, D.C., has provided the following helpful insights regarding the meaning of "rest of God" in Hebrews 4:

> Serenity and laughter are the marks of being in the place of rest. The rest of God is not cessation from activity, but a peace within the toil.... Part of what rest means [is] to be at this place, at this time, doing the thing He has planned for us to do, confident in His strength and resources, in the design of the system. This confidence in the foreknowledge and plan of God is a very accurate definition of faith. This faith permits—urges—the believer to move out in obedience.... It is no wonder the writer urges his readers to enter this kind of rest. How many times are hypertension, migraine headaches, a peptic ulcer, arthritis, nervous exhaustion, illness, insomnia, overweight and irascibility evidences of a life not at peace with the will and pace of God?[6]

The writer of Hebrews repeatedly encourages us to take advantage of the window of opportunity called "today" that God gives us in which to receive by faith His rest as a gift and a blessing. There is a danger of missing His rest if we rebel and turn away from Him (see Heb 3:7-11,15; 4:7), if we turn to other false gods or sources of so-called rest that eventually end up as unrest, turmoil, and emptiness.

We will examine in more detail how to experience such spiritual rest in the next few chapters, especially the ones on Shepherd-centeredness, Spirit-filled surrender, solitude and silence, and Sabbath. The balance of the book will explore the four aspects of rest that each one of us desires: physical, emotional, relational, and spiritual. Because these four are interrelated, our eventual experience of rest is a holistic one, integrating all types of rest as the *shalom* or peace of God. To enter into such rest we must begin with Shepherd-centeredness—abiding in Jesus Christ, our Great and Good Shepherd, in the context of a personal, loving, intimate relationship with Him. He is ultimately the secret and the source of all true rest and peace.

*Part Two:*

~

# Experiencing
# Rest

# Three

# Shepherd-Centeredness

Jesus Christ, God the Son, our Lord and Savior, is the secret and source of all true rest and *shalom*. He has many names in the Bible. In this chapter, we will focus on the Lord Jesus as our Shepherd. He is the "Good Shepherd" (Jn 10:11,14) who lays down His life for the sheep, the "Great Shepherd" of the sheep (Heb 13:20) who continues to care for us, and the "Chief Shepherd" (1 Pt 5:4) who will come again with eternal rewards that will never fade away. As a shepherd does with sheep, so our Lord Jesus as our Shepherd will lead us, protect us, feed us, nurture us, comfort us, and protect us as His sheep. He wants us to experience deeply true spiritual rest by turning to Him and trusting His saving grace and loving care for us.

### Making the Lord Our Shepherd: Psalm 23

The Twenty-third Psalm is one of the most loved and well-known psalms in the Bible. It has been called "The Shepherd Psalm" by F.B. Meyer.[1] A closer look at this psalm will help us better understand how to turn to Jesus and trust and obey Him: there really is no other way to be happy in Jesus (and be at rest), as the hymn says, but to trust and obey Him.

David stated in Psalm 23:1: "The Lord is my shepherd, I shall not be in want." The secret of a contented life of rest that will not be in want or lacking in what we really need is to make the Lord Himself our own Shepherd. The first and most crucial question we should ask ourselves is, "Is the Lord *my* Shepherd?" In other words, have you given your life over to Him and received Jesus Christ personally into your heart, by faith through prayer, as your own Lord and Savior? As *your* Shepherd? Remember, He is the Good Shepherd who gave His life for us and died for us on the cross at Calvary two thousand years ago and rose from the dead so that we may be saved—so that we may become His sheep (see Jn 10). In Isaiah 53:6 we read, "We all, like sheep, have gone astray, each of us has turned to his own way; and the Lord has laid on him the iniquity of us all." Jesus took the weight of our sin, or iniquity, on the cross, where He died in our place—so that we may be saved from our sin and the consequence of eternal death (see Rom 3:23; 5:8; 6:23).

The turmoil, emptiness, unrest, and restlessness of our world, and in our own souls, are often symptoms of our fallen, sinful condition. Saint Augustine's famous quote rings with reality and truth: "Thou hast made us for Thyself and our souls are restless until they find their rest in Thee." I believe it was Pascal who similarly pointed out that in every human heart there is a God-shaped vacuum only God can fill—because it is God-shaped! We are restless until we find our rest in the Lord as *our* Shepherd. We are empty until we are filled with Him in our hearts. The Lord Jesus is the secret of true spiritual rest and fulfillment! The first step in Shepherd-centeredness and entering into God's rest is therefore to turn to Jesus and accept Him into our hearts by faith as our Lord and Savior and Shepherd, trusting Him to forgive us our sins—and to give us the peace of God that is beyond all understanding!

I took this first step of Shepherd-centeredness leading to the experience of God's rest and peace over thirty years ago. I was a young teenager then in Singapore, my country of origin. Although I had many friends, did very well academically in school, played lots of soccer, ran in long-distance events, and had a good family and friendly neighbors, I felt empty deep inside my soul. In particular I had a real fear of death. Questions such as "Where did I come from?" "Why am I here?" "Where am I going after I die?" were excruciatingly painful and very real to my young mind and heart. I experienced the restlessness Augustine described and the God-shaped vacuum or void of emptiness that Pascal wrote about. I went through several months of soul-searching, seeking for substantial answers to my deepest longings. I realize now that I was "homesick for Eden," as Gary Moon would put it,[2] homesick for God Himself.

By His grace and mercy alone, and not by any merit of mine, the Lord reached out to me. He allowed two accidents to happen in which I ended up with a broken left arm—twice in the same place! The first accident occurred in June 1968, when I fell off a small bicycle and broke my arm. Two months later, I slipped off a mossy pavement near the beach and fell, only to break my arm in the same place a second time!—just when it was almost fully healed from the first accident. It was not only physically painful but emotionally and spiritually devastating. I really came to the end of my rope, so to speak, and was more desperate for answers than ever before.

Dallas Willard, at a RENOVARE (Spiritual Renewal) International Conference held in Houston, Texas, in July 1999, made a profound remark, as he often does, in response to the question, "Where can God be found; what is His address?" As I recall, Dallas said, "God's address is always at the end of your rope. He can always be found there!" How true!

So at the end of my rope, with an arm twice broken, I still remember clearly how I gave my life to Jesus that August night in 1968. A couple of my neighbors who were Christians had been sharing the gospel of Jesus Christ with me and challenged me to become a Christian by receiving Jesus into my heart as my personal Lord and Savior. I had always believed in God, and in Jesus too in some vague way, since I attended a Roman Catholic school, had taken catechism classes, and had gone to some church services. However, that night, with tears streaming down my cheeks, I looked out into a beautiful star-studded sky and felt the tug of the Good Shepherd Himself. He was calling me to come home to Him. I finally prayed with all my heart. I asked the Lord Jesus to come into my life and be my Lord and Savior, to forgive me my sins, to show me what life is all about, and to give me His answer to my fear of death. Nothing dramatic happened that night. I went to bed and slept.

The next morning I awoke with a deep peace and rest in my heart that I had never experienced before. My arm was still broken, but I knew something very deep had taken place in my soul. The Lord had come into my heart as I asked Him to: He became *my* Shepherd and has been and will be all my life unto eternity! My fear of death was gone. I had become a Christian, a disciple of Jesus, and so I am today. I was broken but made whole by Him! I told my neighbors and they were overjoyed. They brought me to their church, where I experienced the deep joy of fellowship with other Christians and worship of God.

I grew quickly in Christ with their help and the regular

practice of spiritual disciplines such as prayer and Scripture reading, meditation, and memorization. I had begun to enter into God's rest by becoming a Christian. This is always the first step in Shepherd-centeredness, which leads to true rest. Our hearts *are* restless until they find their rest in God, in the Lord our Shepherd. I experienced peace with God (Rom 5:1) as well as the peace of God (Phil 4:7) through receiving Jesus Christ into my heart by faith (Rom 5:1).

With the Lord Himself as *our* own Shepherd, the rest of Psalm 23 is also ours to claim as He ministers to us thus:

He makes me lie down in green pastures, he leads me beside quiet waters,

he restores my soul. He guides me in paths of righteousness for his name's sake.

Even though I walk through the valley of the shadow of death, I will fear no evil, for you are with me; your rod and your staff, they comfort me.

You prepare a table before me in the presence of my enemies. You anoint my head with oil; my cup overflows.

Surely goodness and love will follow me all the days of my life, and I will dwell in the house of the Lord forever.

PSALM 23:2-6

F.B. Meyer has noted that Psalm 23:2 breathes the very spirit or essence of rest and can be translated as follows: "He maketh me to lie down in pastures of tender grass: He leadeth me beside the waters of rest."[3] In commenting on this verse, he wrote, "We all need rest. There must be pauses and parentheses in our lives.... But there is no part of our nature that cries more urgently for rest than our spiritual life. The spirit of man, like the dove, cannot always be wandering with unresting wing; it must alight.... We must be able to lie down in green pastures or to pass gently along the waters of rest."[4]

Meyer mentioned three things that are required for sheep or human spirits to rest: (1) a consciousness of safety (see Rom 8:34; Jn 10:28; Ps 121:5; 1 Jn 5:18); (2) sufficiency of food (see Jn 6:35); and (3) obedience to the Shepherd's lead (see Jn 10:27). He concluded, "Oh, sigh not for the rest of God as if it were impossible for you! The Good Shepherd wants to make you lie down, and to give you to drink long drafts of rest. Only trust Him! Hand over to Him all that breaks the stillness of your spirit, though it be but a gnat sting; and take from Him His own deep, sweet rest."[5]

### Abiding in Christ: John 15:5

The first step to Shepherd-centeredness in Christ is to receive Him into our hearts. The second step is to abide in Him, to remain in Him, to continue to be centered in Him, for without Him or apart from Him we can do nothing! John 15:5 teaches this truth clearly: "I am the vine, you are the branches. He who abides in Me, and I in him, bears much fruit; for without Me you can do nothing" (NKJV). The NIV for John 15:5 reads, "I am the vine; you are the branches. If a man remains in me and I in him, he will bear much fruit; apart from me you can do nothing." Eugene Peterson in *The Message* renders John 15:5 this way: "I am the Vine, you are the branches. When you're joined with me and I with you, the relation intimate and organic, the harvest is sure to be abundant. Separated, you can't produce a thing."[6]

The Lord, *our* Shepherd, wants us to abide or remain in Him, to continue to be in an intimate, close relationship with Him. This is the secret of abundant fruit-bearing spiritually, whether becoming more Christlike (Rom 8:29) and producing the fruit of the Spirit, such as love, joy, peace, patience, kindness, goodness, faithfulness, gentleness, and self-control (Gal 5:22-23), or producing an abundant harvest of souls won to Christ. We can do or produce nothing without Him. Abiding in a loving, intimate, close relationship with Jesus is therefore essential to experiencing rest and peace as part of the fruit of the Spirit. Abiding in Christ is a crucial part of Shepherd-centeredness. It requires much time spent alone with Him and in His Word, in deep fellowship and relationship with Him, a topic that will be covered in more depth in the chapter on solitude and silence.

### Rest in Jesus Himself Through Surrender and Meekness: Matthew 11:28-30

Finally, it is really important to realize that ultimately it is *Jesus Himself* who gives us true rest for our souls, based on Matthew 11:28-30. *He* actually is our rest! He invites us to come to *Him* and *He* will give us rest. Donald Hagner made the following comments on this text: "Jesus now promises to those who come to him and follow him in discipleship: *he* will give them rest for their souls, i.e., a realization of a deep existential peace, a *shalom*, or sense of ultimate well-being with regard to one's relationship to God and his commandments."[7] Jesus also promises us His peace, and He is our peace in the midst of a world of trouble or tribulation (see Jn 14:27; 16:33).

Darrell Johnson, then senior pastor of Glendale Presbyterian

Church in Glendale, California, and director of chapel at Fuller Theological Seminary, preached on this text at the Fuller Faculty Retreat in September 1998. He rendered Matthew 11:28 thus: "Come to me all you who labor and have overburdened yourselves, and *I will rest you,*" emphasizing that only Jesus can give us true rest and He is our rest. With reference to Matthew 11:29, Johnson paraphrased it this way: *"I will put your souls at rest—by taking my yoke upon you."* He noted that Jesus does not ask us to yoke with Him but rather to wear the yoke that He wears! Soul-rest or refreshment of soul comes from such a transfer of yoke. What then is Jesus' yoke? Johnson suggested that if we begin with Matthew 11:25 rather than Matthew 11:28 and see the larger context of this passage in Scripture, we will see that the yoke Jesus wears is *His filial relationship with God the Father.* In other words, it is the yoke of intimate fellowship with God, and this yoke is easy and light! This is the secret of rest, and this is the MAIN thing in life. As Stephen Covey, Roger Merrill, and Rebecca Merrill wrote in their well-known book *First Things First:* "THE MAIN THING IS TO KEEP THE MAIN THING THE MAIN THING!"[8]

Jesus is therefore inviting us, calling us, into the main thing of an intimate, close relationship with God as the basis of true soul-rest, which only He can offer us. To be Shepherd-centered, then, is always to focus on Jesus and take upon ourselves His blessed yoke of deep fellowship with a loving God, who has a perfect Father-heart of caring and compassion for us as His children.

Jesus does not just give us rest, but *He Himself is* our rest. Wayne Barber, in his book *The Rest of Grace* on entering into the wonder of the Christ life, described how he used to feel about his Christian walk: there was a piece missing. Although he tried his hardest to do the right thing, such as loving people, he ended up frustrated and defeated. Then one day, by God's grace and through His Word, he realized that he was still trying to do it himself. In his own words: "My striving was of the flesh, and as I read my Bible it dawned on me that was the very reason God had sent His Spirit into my life—to give me rest from my own fleshly striving. Christ didn't just give me life, He *is* my life. He empowers me to do what He knows I cannot do without Him."[9] Commenting on Matthew 11:28-30, he wrote, "Here I had been trying to do the work myself, and Jesus was telling me to rest in Him.... That's the message of grace. When we learn that Christ is our life, we can *rest* in His grace.... Christ is your life, and you need nothing else—let the joy of His power give you the rest you've been seeking."[10]

Richard Swenson has called the rest Jesus offers in Matthew 11:28-30 "surrendered rest."[11] Jesus Himself gives us rest and is our rest, but we experience Him and such rest only as we learn to surrender to Him in meekness and humility. A.W. Tozer put it this way:

> To men and women everywhere Jesus says, "Come unto me, and I will give you rest." The rest He offers is the rest of meekness, the blessed relief which comes when we accept ourselves for what we are and cease to pretend. It will take some courage at first, but the needed grace will come as we learn that we are sharing this new and easy yoke with the strong Son of God Himself....
>
> *Lord, make me childlike. Deliver me from the urge to compete with another for place or prestige or position. I would be simple and artless as a little child. Deliver me from pose and*

*pretense.... Help me to forget myself and find my true peace in beholding Thee.... Lay upon me Thy easy yoke of self-forgetfulness that through it I may find rest. Amen.*[12]

In the next chapter, we will discuss more fully Spirit-filled surrender, or how to yield to the presence and power of the Holy Spirit, who enables us to remain Shepherd-centered and thus to continue experiencing God's rest.

*Four*

≈

# Spirit-Filled Surrender

Submit. Yield. Surrender. These are words that are almost alien or unacceptable in our vocabulary today. In our fast-paced, accelerated, high-tech world, the buzzwords that are "in" include: Stand Up, Assert Yourself, Speak Out, Look Out for Number One, You, Talk Back, You Have Rights, You Are Entitled to _____! In the midst of our self-centered, self-preoccupied, self-indulgent, and self-serving society, Jesus turns our world upside down by teaching us that the secret to deep soul-rest is to surrender to Him in meekness and humility (Mt 11:28-30), as we learned in the last chapter. He calls us to true discipleship, following Him all the way with all of our hearts, by denying ourselves and taking up our cross *daily* (Lk 9:23). He wisely and profoundly warns us, "For whoever wants to save his life will lose it, but whoever loses his life for me will save it. What good is it for a man to gain the whole world, and yet lose or forfeit his very self?" (Lk 9:24-25).

Experiencing God's rest in Jesus requires such daily, moment-by-moment walking with Him, in full surrender to Him by yielding to the Holy Spirit's presence and power in our lives, by continually being filled with the Spirit (Eph 5:18). Christians trying to be more like Jesus are familiar with the letters WWJD: What Would Jesus Do? This is a good question to ask, but what may be more crucial and biblical is to realize that WWJD means Walking With Jesus Daily—in Spirit-filled or Spirit-controlled surrender! That way we will unselfconsciously become more and more like Jesus as the Holy Spirit transforms us into greater conformity to Christ (Rom 8:29), or as Christ is formed in us (Gal 4:19).

In order to understand more about Spirit-filled surrender, let us consider the following questions in more depth: What do we surrender? To whom do we surrender? How do we surrender?

## What Do We Surrender?

A few years ago, David Daniels, then pastor of collegiate ministries at First Evangelical Free Church in Austin, Texas, wrote about a real-life experience he had during a one-day prayer retreat. He had decided to have a prayer retreat once a month. Anticipating an entire day of simply enjoying the wonderful presence of the Lord, he drove to his retreat site only twenty miles from home. He ended up in a chapel by a small river. Here is part of his story in his own words:

> I began by asking God to open the doors to Heaven so that I could enjoy Him in prayer and worship. Then I read Scripture. I meditated on certain passages. I quoted verses and memorized new ones. I prayed. I sang hymns aloud. I prayed some more. And I wept.
>
> Five hours into my day, my joyful anticipation had turned to bitter frustration. I paced the aisles, angry with God

because, though I was drawing near to Him, He seemed so far away from me....

His message was undeniably clear: "My child, I'm not hiding from you. You've been hiding from Me. And before you can enjoy fellowship with Me, you must uncover the hidden places of your heart."

The words were indicting but true. I harbored sin—habits, words, actions, attitudes—that I had tried to conceal.... It was time to be honest with God.

That day, I learned that *communion with God must be preceded by confession before God.*[1]

This is what we need to surrender first to God: our sin. We need to confess our sinfulness and our specific sins to Him. The psalmist says in Psalm 66:18, "If I had cherished sin in my heart, the Lord would not have listened." David Daniels learned the truth of this verse when he concluded that confession before God must come first before communion with God.

Unconfessed sin in our lives does not only break our communion with God; it also results in restlessness or unrest, like the tossing sea with its waves. In Isaiah 57:20-21 we read, "But the wicked are like the tossing sea, which cannot rest, whose waves cast up mire and mud. 'There is no peace,' says my God, 'for the wicked'" (also see Is 48:22).

Sin is always, ultimately, destructive to us as persons, and to our experience of soul-rest (see 1 Pt 2:11), although it may be pleasurable for a short time (Heb 11:25). It is never worth it at all!

In a recent powerful and challenging book, *Go and Sin No More,* Michael Brown, president of the Brownsville Revival School of Ministry in Pensacola, Florida, wrote:

Several years ago, after preaching one night in Kuopio, Finland, I spent the early hours of the morning with the Lord. In close communion with Him, I wrote down this simple prayer: "Lord, help me to hate sin in my life as mercilessly as I judge it in the lives of others." Would that all of us lived this out! It would change many of our lives dramatically. And when we realize that *God hates sin*—acutely, passionately, totally—we have more than enough reason to flee from that which defiles and cleave to that which is good, pure, and wholesome—in other words, to that which is holy and to Him who is holy. It is for Him, through Him, and to Him that we are holy—Let's pursue His call![2]

In 1 Peter 1:15-16, we read, "But just as he who called you is holy, so be holy in all you do; for it is written: 'Be holy because I am holy.'" To be holy is not only to be set apart *from* sin and impurity but also to be set apart *to* God—in full surrender to Him and to moral purity. We are further challenged in 1 Peter 2:11, "Dear friends, I urge you, as aliens and strangers in the world, to abstain from sinful desires, which war against your soul." And in Colossians 3:5-6, "Put to death, therefore, whatever belongs to your earthly nature: sexual immorality, impurity, lust, evil desires and greed, which is idolatry. Because of these, the wrath of God is coming."

In Sergio Scataglini's recent book on the fire of God's holiness and how he was powerfully touched by such fire, he challenges us with God's call to 100 percent holiness or purity:

[God] told me: "Nobody gets up in the morning and prepares a cup of coffee, puts just one drop of poison in it, then stirs and drinks it." He revealed that many people in the church allow poison into their hearts and minds. Without a doubt, this small quota of sin is destroying them. No one would consider buying a bottle of mineral water with a label that reads: "98% Pure Mineral Water, 2% Sewage Water." Yet many Christians have allowed spiritual sewage water to seep into their lives.[3]

In writing this chapter, the Lord stopped me right in the middle of it and spoke to me personally about sin and specific sins in my life. I could not continue writing and so went into a bedroom and knelt by the bed before Him. I wept and confessed my sinfulness and sins to Him as the Holy Spirit convicted me anew and more deeply. But He gave me a godly sorrow in genuine repentance, which led to tears of joy and rest in Him as I experienced afresh His forgiveness and tender love for me. He is calling me to deeper, 100 percent holiness so that I can know Him more fully and be filled more completely with the *Holy* Spirit!

In confessing our basic sinfulness and deceitfulness of heart (Jer 17:9) in true repentance with godly sorrow for having grieved the Lord, and not worldly sorrow that leads to death (2 Cor 7:9-10), it will be helpful to take inventory of our specific sins as well. The ancient list of the seven deadly sins is as good a place to start as any: pride, avarice (or greed), envy, sloth (or laziness), lust (or lasciviousness), gluttony, and anger. Unfortunately, most Americans do not view the seven deadly sins as sin at all or as sin that is deadly! Carol Tavris, a psychologist and author, spoke on the subject of pride some years ago at the American Psychological Association's Annual Convention in August 1985 in Los Angeles. She made the following insightful comments:

Given the typically high expectations of Americans—their excess pride—some sort of failure is almost inevitable. Yet psychologists don't like to study how people handle failure, even though an understanding of how people fail gracefully could help them to grow.

Of the seven deadly sins, gluttony is the only sin still recognized by American society.... The others have acquired a certain respectability.

Avarice today is disguised as Reagonomics. Envy is marketed as a "motivating factor." Sloth is marketed as stress management. Lust is stage one of the sexual cycle. Anger is a healthy response. And pride has been downgraded to "self-esteem."[4]

We may chuckle at these comments, but they do reveal the deceitfulness of human hearts in rationalizing away sin that grieves the Lord and harms us in the long run. It would do our souls great good if we would simply confess, with deep repentance, our sins of pride, avarice (or greed), envy, sloth, lust, gluttony, and anger (of the wrong kind and not righteous indignation) where applicable.

Richard Foster, in a more contemporary mode, has focused on three major areas: money, sex, and power. He has described the demon in money as greed, the demon in sex as lust, and the demon in power as pride.[5] In fact, pride in particular needs to be confessed and surrendered to God. Pride is sin (Prv 21:4), and God hates pride and arrogance (Prv 6:16-17; 8:13; 16:5). Pride is forbidden in Scripture (for example, see 1 Sm 2:3; Rom 12:3, 16), and we are warned that pride goes before destruction or a fall (Prv 16:18). I believe it was C.S. Lewis who pointed out that pride is what leads to every other vice, and as a spiritual cancer pride eats up the very possibility of love or contentment. G.K. Chesterton apparently said that if he could preach just once, he would preach a sermon against pride. Pride does not lead to rest—it leads to much unrest and restlessness (see Hb 2:5) and eventually to destruction. Jesus teaches us instead to walk the way of meekness and humility that leads to Himself and to true soul-rest (Mt 11:29). In Psalm 51:17 we read the words of David: "The sacrifices of God are a broken spirit; a broken and contrite heart, O God, you will not despise." Brokenness, in genuine repentance, which leads to 100 percent holiness, is the secret to peace and God's rest and deep joy!

Besides confessing our sinfulness as well as specific sins in genuine repentance (which cares more about having hurt and grieved the Lord deeply than about being caught or feeling guilty and wanting to feel better *ourselves* or being afraid of punishment or dire consequences), what else do we surrender?

We should also surrender or yield *every* area of our lives to God, to the lordship of Christ: our time, talents (gifts or skills), treasure (money and possessions), relationships, and more. Everything that we are or have has come from the Lord and belongs to Him (see 1 Chr 29:11-14). It makes sense to surrender gratefully and lovingly every area of our lives to Him and His loving control and lordship. The Lord Jesus has also bought or redeemed us with His precious blood, and we are no longer our own: we belong to Him as the temple or dwelling place of the Holy Spirit (1 Cor 6:19-20). As we have received Jesus Christ as Lord, we should continue to live in Him (Col 2:6), as Lord of *every* area of our lives. Although we are not perfect, we need to remember that partial obedience or delayed obedience to the Lord is still disobedience and sin. Yet He is very patient and compassionate toward us, wooing us with His love so that we will trust and obey Him more as we surrender more of our lives to Him.

Finally, the Lord wants us to surrender our very *hearts:* ourselves, or our souls, fully to Him and to Him alone. In Proverbs 23:26 we read, "My son, give me your heart and let your eyes keep to my ways." The greatest commandment according to Jesus is to love the Lord our God with all our heart, with all our soul, with all our mind, and with all our strength, and then to love our neighbor as ourself (Mk 12:30-31). The first priority always is to love the Lord—with all that we are: emotionally, spiritually, intellectually, and physically. With our whole heart. With our whole being. We surrender our very self to Him. We give Him our hearts. It makes sense! After all, He has already given His whole heart and His whole life for us.

Surrendering our hearts to God means loving Him and worshiping Him alone, above all others: He is supreme and number one. The Lord Jesus should have the supremacy or preeminence in *everything* (Col 1:18). The danger in our lives is to be seduced by "lesser gods." Leslie Williams has written about life, love, even church, and other dangerous idols in her book on the seduction of the lesser gods. Even so-called good things can displace the Lord from being the center of our hearts. In her own words:

> What does it mean to worship lesser gods?... As humans, we are tempted in a variety of ways, but idolatry tempts us to put something other than God at the center of our lives. We live this out by devoting our best energies, the bulk of our time ... to anything (people, ideas, or objects) other than the Lord.
>
> This displacement of God is what I mean by "worshiping" lesser gods....

Worshiping other gods often catches us off guard, our lives slipping out of proportion before we know what's happened. How does it happen, for instance, that I come to love my job more than God? When does the need to control my children become more important than God's will for them? Why am I suddenly consumed with too much church work and not enough worship time? The enemy is sneaky and persistent and delights every time we give our best to anything other than God Himself. The heart of idolatry is really selfishness.... This misplaced loyalty is the lie of Satan, and we must learn to resist.[6]

To give God our heart also means that we need to let go of our ego, our selfish or egocentric false, sinful self. Ken Blanchard, Bill Hybels, and Phil Hodges in a recent book defined EGO as to *Edge God Out!*[7] Sue Monk Kidd has written with deep insight on the need to overcome superficial or quickaholic spirituality by learning to wait and *stay* in the waiting process in order to truly grow spiritually. This will involve letting go of our ego or false self in order to find our true self in Christ. She wrote:

In order for the ego to relinquish its central position, my hardened structures must be cracked open. This process opens a way for the gradual shift of centers, a deep restructuring away from the ruling needs of the ego toward the self, or core of God within.... In Christian language, this is plain, old-fashioned surrender—giving up our conscious will and striving, and yielding to the inner kingdom.[8]

During a visit to the Abbey of Gethsemane and Thomas Merton's hermitage, she learned from Brother Anthony that the whole point or purpose is to let go and to be still, because this is what opens us to the deep center of God's presence within us. In letting go, we learn to wait with God.[9] We learn therefore to surrender our hearts to Him.

## To Whom Do We Surrender?

It is obvious by now that we surrender or yield our hearts or whole beings to the Triune God: Father, Son, and Holy Spirit. However, I want to emphasize in this chapter the need to surrender particularly to the control of the Holy Spirit. We are commanded in Ephesians 5:18 to continually be filled with the Spirit: to be "empowered, released, guided, and controlled" by the Holy Spirit.[10] We need the Spirit's presence and power in order to experience God's rest and peace. Part of the fruit of the Spirit is peace (Gal 5:22-23). Spirit-filled surrender means that it is the Holy Spirit who enables and empowers us to yield or surrender to God, and as we surrender, the Spirit fills us and empowers us even more! It is a blessed cycle, ever deepening, of Spirit-filled surrender!

Bill Bright, founder and president of Campus Crusade for Christ International, wrote the following in his foreword to Michael Brown's book *Go and Sin No More*:

> Personal holiness is the key to God's ultimate plans for us all.... How can we be holy? In ourselves, we cannot. We can only do so by the ministry of the Holy Spirit within us.... We cannot effectively do anything, even witness for Christ, without the enabling and power of the Holy Spirit.... Of course, God has given us a free will, and therefore we must be willing to cooperate with Him. We must *choose* to be filled with the Spirit. We must *choose* to allow the Holy Spirit to be in control of our lives.[11]

We therefore choose to surrender to the Holy Spirit, and He will lead us into a more intimate and loving relationship with God the Father and Jesus Christ the Son, so that we end up having a special communion with and within the community of the Triune God: Father, Son, and Holy Spirit. We surrender to God Himself in Three Persons.

## How Do We Surrender?

Bill Bright has a simple but helpful answer to our question of how we surrender to God: "I like to think of life in Christ in terms of 'spiritual breathing.' I *exhale* by confessing any known sin. Then I *inhale*, surrendering control of my life to Christ and receiving the fullness of the Holy Spirit by faith."[12] We surrender to God by such basic spiritual breathing—day by day, moment by moment. It involves yielding or submitting to the Holy Spirit's presence and power: being filled with the Spirit, so that He is not just Resident in our hearts (all Christians have the Holy Spirit indwelling them—see 1 Cor 12:13) but President of our lives! So that Jesus Christ is Lord of every area of our lives!

In an earlier book I coauthored with Douglas Gregg, *Disciplines of the Holy Spirit*, we described five steps to being filled with the Spirit as we surrender to Him:

First, confess your sins and receive God's cleansing and forgiveness by the blood of Christ (1 Jn 1:9).... Second, yield every area of your life to the control of the Holy Spirit, under the Lordship of Jesus Christ (Rom 12:1-2).... Third, ask! In obedience to the command in Ephesians 5:18, ask to be filled with the Holy Spirit.... Fourth, give thanks. Thank God by faith for his answer to such prayers because they are in accordance with his will (1 Jn 5:14-15).... Fifth, expect great things to happen. Anticipate that the Holy Spirit will work deeply and powerfully, whether in dramatic or in more quiet ways.[13]

The following is an example of how we can pray in Spirit-filled surrender on a daily basis, so that we can experience more of the presence and power of the Holy Spirit as He fills us in answer to such prayer:

> *Dear Father, thank you for your love for me. I want to confess my sins to you as specifically as possible....*
>
> *I am sorry for grieving you. I know I have hurt you by doing things that are wrong and that displease you. I thank you that by the blood of Jesus Christ I can now receive your forgiveness and cleansing.*
>
> *I want to yield to you every area of my life, including those areas where I might have strayed, and I do so now....*
>
> *I pray, in the name of Jesus, that you will fill me with the presence and power of the Holy Spirit, that you will enable me today to become more like Jesus and to do what will glorify you, touch lives, and bring people closer to you. I commit to you all the events of this day ... I ask that you will glorify yourself through me today and draw me closer to you.*
>
> *Thank you, Lord. In Jesus' name. Amen.*[14]

This is the kind of prayer of surrender and for the filling of the Holy Spirit that I pray as I begin each day of my life with the Lord, and as I go on throughout the day walking with Him.

Andrew Murray wrote about such surrender as "absolute surrender."[15] It is the only way to experience the fullness of God's true rest: absolute or full surrender to God alone. David learned this precious truth many years ago, and he wrote, "My soul finds rest in God alone; my salvation comes from him. He alone is my rock and my salvation; he is my fortress, I will never be shaken.... Find rest, O my soul, in God alone; my hope comes from him. He alone is my rock and my salvation; he is my fortress, I will not be shaken" (Ps 62:1-2, 5-6).

# Five

# Solitude and Silence

"Without solitude it is virtually impossible to live a spiritual life," wrote Henri Nouwen.[1] Similarly, Dallas Willard has emphasized the centrality and significance of solitude among the spiritual disciplines available to help us grow spiritually: "Solitude frees us actually. This above all explains its primacy and priority among the disciplines.... Solitude is generally the most fundamental in the beginning of the spiritual life, and it must be returned to again and again as that life develops."[2] In order to follow Christ in deed as a true disciple, living in every aspect of life as Jesus lived, Willard writes, "activities such as solitude, silence, fasting, prayer, service, celebration—disciplines for life in the spiritual kingdom of God and activities in which Jesus deeply immersed himself—are essential to the deliverance of human beings from the concrete power of sin and ... they can make the experience of the easy yoke a reality in life."[3]

Solitude is basically spending time alone by yourself, to be with God, deliberately withdrawing from all human contact or interaction. It is a crucial spiritual discipline that enables us, by the power of the Holy Spirit, to be freed from bondage to things or people, especially people's opinions and evaluations of us. Silence, the absence of words or speech and other sounds like music and noise, is a key component of solitude.[4]

It is interesting to note that even in a more secular context, Ester Schaler Buchholz recently wrote a book entitled *The Call of Solitude*, emphasizing the human need for alone time or solitude (time by yourself) in a world of attachment.[5] Drawing on biology, anthropology, philosophy, literature, and psychoanalysis, she asserted that alone time is an essential biological and developmental need for both children and adults, thus giving permission to people to have the quiet and peace or rest they long for. The description of the book on its jacket cover concludes, "In today's world, where the pace moves at lightning speed, endangering our inner lives, Buchholz's voice is a vital one, calling us to contemplation and rest in a world that is too much with us."

A world that is too much with us. Where attachment to human beings or relationships may be overemphasized. The need for solitude or alone time in general is therefore even more acute today. More specifically, the need for solitude and silence as spiritual disciplines in the Christian life is crucial. As noted earlier, John Ortberg's wise mentor told him, in answer to his question about how to be spiritually healthy, *"You must ruthlessly eliminate hurry from your life."* An essential means for eliminating hurry and experiencing more of God's rest and peace is practicing the spiritual disciplines of solitude and silence.

## The Secret of Transforming Power

Jesus lived a busy life on earth, where He ministered to many people: teaching and preaching the good news of the kingdom of God, healing the sick, feeding the hungry, and casting out demons from those who were demonized. The Gospels in the New Testament provide clear and powerful accounts of these works and words of Jesus as the Messiah, the Savior and Lord of humankind. What was the secret of such transforming power in His life and ministry?

There are several passages in the Bible that give us an answer to this key question. For example, in Luke 5:15-16 we read, "Yet the news about him spread all the more, so that crowds of people came to hear him and to be healed of their sicknesses. But Jesus often withdrew to lonely places and prayed." In the midst of a busy and full schedule of ministry to people, including teaching and preaching as well as healing, Jesus deliberately or intentionally withdrew Himself from people, to go to lonely places, deserted or solitary places in the wilderness—and prayed. He regularly practiced the spiritual disciplines of solitude and silence, and prayer. He had alone time on a frequent basis, to commune deeply with the Father, in the Spirit.

Another instance in Scripture where we find Jesus in solitude and prayer is in Mark 1:35. The preceding verses in the text show Jesus again busy in healing many sick people of their various diseases and driving out many demons (Mk 1:32-34). In the midst of all this intense ministry, we read of Him in Mark 1:35, "Very early in the morning, while it was still dark, Jesus got up, left the house and went off to a solitary place, where he prayed." The secret of transforming power in His life and ministry was regular times of solitude and prayer that connected

Him intimately in communion with the Father.

Nouwen wrote the following helpful words based on Mark 1:35:

> In the center of breathless activities we hear a restful breathing. Surrounded by hours of moving we find a moment of quiet stillness. In the heart of much involvement there are words of withdrawal. In the midst of action there is contemplation. And after much togetherness there is solitude. The more I read this nearly silent sentence locked in between the loud words of action, the more I have the sense that the secret of Jesus' ministry is hidden in that lonely place where he went to pray, early in the morning. Long before dawn.
>
> In the lonely place Jesus finds the courage to follow God's will and not his own; to speak God's words and not his own; to do God's work and not his own ... (Jn 5:30 ... Jn 14:10).... It is in the lonely place, where Jesus enters into intimacy with the Father, that his ministry is born.
>
> ...The careful balance between silence and words, withdrawal and involvement, distance and closeness, solitude and community forms the basis of the Christian life.[6]

Jesus therefore calls us as His disciples to follow Him in the practice of solitude and silence that includes prayer, as He did with the early disciples in Mark 6:31: "Then, because so many people were coming and going that they did not even have a chance to eat, he said to them, 'Come with me by yourselves to a quiet place and get some rest.'" In the old King James Version this verse is translated as "Come ... apart into a desert place, and rest a while." One pastor I know commented that we need to come apart and rest awhile or we will simply come apart! My version of this loving warning is to take a break or risk having a breakdown! It is pure wisdom to obey the Lord's call to solitude and rest, especially in the midst of a busy and intense, even hectic time of ministry. As we deliberately choose to withdraw from interaction with people in order to be alone with the Lord in solitude, He will give us rest.

Eugene Peterson in *The Message* has given us a contemporary and clear rendering of Matthew 11:28-30 that speaks directly to our hearts and our deepest longings for rest: "Are you tired? Worn out? Burned out on religion? Come to me. Get away with me and you'll recover your life. I'll show you how to take a real rest. Walk with me and work with me—watch how I do it. Learn the unforced rhythms of grace. I won't lay anything heavy or ill-fitting on you. Keep company with me and you'll learn to live freely and lightly."[7]

Eugene Peterson puts it beautifully: We are to walk with Jesus and work with Him, learning from Him by watching how He does it. Learning especially "the unforced rhythms of grace." Reading the Gospels in particular will give us a much clearer picture of this.

## Growing in Grace

In solitude and silence, in communion with Jesus or prayer, we will come to understand and experience grace much more deeply. J.I. Packer has defined grace thus:

Grace is God's undeserved favor, His unmerited Love. The word "grace" expresses the thought of God acting in spontaneous goodness to save sinners: God loving the unlovely, making covenant with them, pardoning their sins, accepting their persons, revealing Himself to them, moving them to response, leading them ultimately into full knowledge and enjoyment of Himself, and overcoming all obstacles to the fulfillment of this purpose that at each stage arise.[8]

Grace has been more simply spelled as <u>G</u>od's <u>R</u>iches <u>A</u>t <u>C</u>hrist's <u>E</u>xpense! He paid it all for us—grace is God's pure goodness and love toward us, unmerited, undeserved, unearned. We actually deserve punishment for our sin but He gives us His love and goodness and salvation through Christ instead: This is grace!

Philip Yancey, in his excellent book *What's So Amazing About Grace?* wrote these moving and radical words about grace:

> *Grace means there is nothing we can do to make God love us more*—no amount of spiritual calisthenics and renunciations, no amount of knowledge gained from seminaries and divinity schools, no amount of crusading on behalf of righteous causes. *And grace means there is nothing we can do to make God love us less*—no amount of racism or pride or pornography or adultery or even murder. Grace means that God already loves us as much as an infinite God can possibly love.[9]

As we experience more of God's grace, radical and transforming grace that is so amazing, we will become more "graced" people—more kind, gentle, loving, compassionate, tender, giving, and forgiving. We will, by the power of the Holy Spirit, produce the fruit of the Spirit (Gal 5:22-23): we will become people characterized by love, joy, and peace. People of rest and contentment in Him!

The apostle Paul says in 2 Corinthians 9:8, "And God is able to make all grace abound to you, so that in all things at all times, having all that you need, you will abound in every good work." God is able to do this, and He will make all grace abound to you so that you will abound in every good work! Such grace is often most deeply experienced in our weakness. Again Paul writes in 2 Corinthians 12:9, "But he said to me, 'My grace is sufficient for you, for my power is made perfect in weakness.' Therefore I will boast all the more gladly about my weaknesses, so that Christ's power may rest on me."

### The Struggles in Solitude and Silence

Weakness and struggle are often exposed best in solitude and silence. We face ourselves most honestly in solitude, alone with the Lord. This can be difficult and even frightening for us, but is essential if we are to grow strong in Christ and learn to rest in Him. In the wise words of Nouwen:

Solitude is not a private therapeutic place. Rather, it is the place of conversion, the place where the old self dies and the new self is born....

In solitude I get rid of my scaffolding: no friends to talk to, no telephone calls to make, no meetings to attend, no music to entertain, no books to distract, just me—naked, vulnerable, weak, sinful, deprived, broken—nothing. It is this nothingness that I have to face in my solitude, a nothingness so dreadful that everything in me wants to run to my friends, my work, and my distractions so that I can forget my nothingness....

That is the struggle. It is the struggle to die to the false self. But the struggle is far, far beyond our own strength.... The wisdom of the desert is that the confrontation with our own frightening nothingness forces us to surrender ourselves totally and unconditionally to the Lord Jesus Christ. Alone, we cannot face "the mystery of iniquity" with impunity. Only Christ can overcome the power of evil. Only in and through him can we survive the trials of solitude.[10]

There are times in solitude that the Lord will lead us to experience what St. John of the Cross has described as "the dark night of the soul" (see Is 50:10). Richard Foster writes:

The "dark night" ... is not something bad or destructive.... The purpose of the darkness is not to punish or afflict us. It is to set us free. It is a divine appointment, a privileged opportunity to draw close to the divine center. St. John calls it "sheer grace."...

What does the dark night of the soul involve? We may have a sense of dryness, aloneness, even lostness. Any overdependence on the emotional life is stripped away. The notion, often heard today, that such experiences should be avoided and that we always should live in peace and comfort, joy, and celebration only betrays the fact that much contemporary experience is surface slush. The dark night is one of the ways God brings us into a hush, a stillness so that he may work an inner transformation upon the soul....

Recognize the dark night for what it is. Be grateful that God is lovingly drawing you away from every distraction so that you can see him clearly. Rather than chafing and fighting, become still and wait. I am not referring here to the dull-

ness to spiritual things that comes as a result of sin or disobedience, but I am speaking of the person who is seeking
hard after God and who harbors no known sin in his heart.[11]

Similarly, J.I. Packer reminds us, "Sooner or later, God's guidance, which brings us out of darkness into light, will also bring
us out of light into darkness. It is part of the way of the cross."[12]

A.W. Tozer has described a process he calls "the ministry of
the night," which is similar to the dark night of the soul:

> To do His supreme work of grace within you, He will take
> away from your heart everything you love most. Everything
> you trust in will go from you. Piles of ashes will lie where
> your most precious treasures used to be....
>
> Slowly you will discover God's love in your suffering. Your
> heart will begin to approve the whole thing. You will learn ...
> the healing action of faith without supporting pleasure. You
> will feel and understand *the ministry of the night*; its power to
> purify, to detach, to humble, to destroy the fear of death, and
> what is more important to you at the moment, the fear of
> life. And you will learn that sometimes pain can do what even
> joy cannot, such as exposing the vanity of earth's trifles and
> filling your heart with longing for the peace of heaven.[13]

The peace of heaven. We can experience God's peace and rest
on earth, but only to a certain extent. Beyond that we long for
the perfect and eternal peace of heaven to come. Meanwhile, on
earth, and in solitude, we may experience struggle and sometimes the dark night of the soul or the ministry of the night.
There may be unrest before rest, struggle before serenity, purifi-
cation before peace. This is the paradoxical working of the Spirit

and the ebb and flow of life itself, even the spiritual life, eternal and abundant, that Jesus came to give us in all of its fullness (Jn 10:10).

In times of the dark night of the soul, we need to resist the temptation to run and hide from facing ourselves honestly before God, the temptation to turn to various distractions and defenses, such as blaming others and God Himself. Instead, the crucial stance to take is to wait upon the Lord, to be still and trust Him, to pray and cast not only our cares but ourselves upon Him. To really trust His grace and mercy. And His timing. He will see us through and make a way for us. His grace *is* sufficient for us in every situation and for all things—including dark nights of the soul. We will eventually experience a deeper rest in Him.

The struggle or suffering of such seasons of darkness in solitude is essential for us so as to learn to have our deepest satisfaction or soul-rest in God and God alone. John Piper has written, *"God is most glorified in us when we are most satisfied in him."*[14]

Elaborating on this theme, Piper continues,

Peter says ... "Since therefore Christ suffered in the flesh, arm yourselves with the same thought" (1 Pt 4:1). The suffering of Christ is a call for a certain mindset toward suffering, namely, that it is normal, and that the path of love and missions will often require it.... Suffering with Christ is not strange; it is your calling, your vocation....

You cannot show the preciousness of a person by being happy with his gifts. Ingratitude will certainly prove that the giver is not loved. But gratitude for gifts does not prove that the *giver* is precious. What proves that the giver is precious is the glad-hearted readiness to leave all his gifts to be with him. This is why suffering is so central in the mission of the church.... Worship means cherishing the preciousness of God above all else, including life itself. It will be very hard to bring the nations to love God from a lifestyle that communicates a love of things. Therefore God ordains in the lives of his messengers that suffering sever our bondage to the world. When joy and love survive this severing, we are fit to say to the nations with authenticity and power: Hope in God.[15]

I am writing this chapter around Thanksgiving Day. This is the season when we count our blessings and even name them one by one so that we can express our gratitude and thanks to God, the Giver of such blessings and gifts to us. Many of my church members, including my wife and me, have learned also to be deeply thankful to God for the trials and sufferings we have experienced because they have helped to prune us, to purify us, to purge us, so that we love and worship Him more. Most of all, as John Piper has put it, we are learning to focus less on the gifts, and even to leave them behind if need be, so that we can truly appreciate, love, adore, and worship the Giver Himself: God alone! We need to thank God for God Himself, our greatest Gift! The Giver is the Gift par excellence. We are learning to have our deepest satisfaction in Him alone and thereby letting God be most glorified in us.

In addition to the struggle and ultimate blessing of the dark night of the soul, there are other blessings that often come in our practice of solitude and silence. For example, as the Holy Spirit leads us into the wilderness of solitude and silence (see Lk 4:1), He prepares us to hear the still, small voice or gentle whisper of God Himself that can only be heard clearly in silence (see

1 Kgs 19:11-13; also see Eccl 5:2-7; Jas 1:19), helps us to grow in intimacy with the Triune God, reveals to us God's character and purpose, and strengthens us for spiritual battle and temptation.[16] How then do we practice solitude and silence, often with prayer and Scripture reading and meditation, on a regular basis?

## The Practice of Solitude and Silence

Before suggesting several concrete ways of practicing solitude and silence, it is well to be reminded by Richard Foster, "Solitude is more a state of mind and heart rather than it is a place. There is a solitude of the heart that can be maintained at all times.... In the midst of noise and confusion we are settled into a deep inner silence. Whether alone or among people, we always carry with us a portable sanctuary of the heart."[17]

In *Disciplines of the Holy Spirit*, Doug Gregg and I made several suggestions for the practice of solitude and silence, which I have adapted as follows:

1. Schedule time to be alone with God on a daily basis. Start with ten to fifteen minutes a day and work up to an hour a day if possible. Most Christians call this their "quiet time," but it is often far from quiet, because it is either rushed or crammed with activities like prayer lists and reading Bible passages that must be covered! Prayer and Bible reading can certainly be part of this time alone with God, but make sure there is some time for silence or quiet waiting upon God to truly listen to His voice and to worship Him (for example, see Ps 27:14; 37:7; 46:10; 130:5-6; Is 30:15, 18; 40:29-31).

2. Choose to be silent for a half-day or even a whole day! Do explain to your spouse, family, or roommates what you're planning to do, to avoid any possible misunderstanding!

Silence can initially be difficult with many distracting thoughts, as well as restlessness. This is normal. Hang in there until your mind and heart finally settle down to a stillness that will lead you into the divine center of God's presence within you, by the power of the Holy Spirit.

3. Choose to listen more than you speak, in both your relationship with God as well as your interactions with other people.

4. Take a half-day to a full-day retreat to spend some significant time alone with God in solitude and silence, perhaps once a month.

5. Take a longer retreat of twenty-four to forty-eight hours (or even up to a week) three to four times a year, in order to have prolonged periods of solitude and silence alone with God.[18]

It is important to note that taking such personal retreats, especially if they last for a couple of days or more, may initially lead to some unexpected or unpleasant experiences. For example, David Runcorn noted that three things always happened to him whenever he went away for a few days of retreat: he kept falling asleep, he had a great appetite for food, and after being in silence for a while he would start feeling very restless and irritable![19] These are not uncommon or abnormal reactions. We can spend some of our solitude time sleeping, eating, and being restless! We need to persevere, however, and soon enough we will adjust and really begin to enjoy such prolonged times of solitude and silence that enable us to grow in deeper intimacy with God and to eventually enter more into His rest and peace.

With regard to having private retreats or prolonged times of solitude, Foster has some very helpful words:

> Jesus needed frequent retreat and solitude to do His work, and yet somehow we think we can get by without the same.

It is time we follow our Leader's lead.

The major thing a private retreat accomplishes is to create an open empty space in our lives. We learn to "waste" time for God. Slowly, we come to hear God's speech in His wondrous, terrible, loving, all-embracing silence. Gently we press into the holy of holies where we are sifted in the stillness. Painfully, we let go of the vain images of ourselves that seemed so essential. Joyfully, we loosen our grip on all those projects that appeared so significant.

Most wonderful of all is the empowerment we receive: overcoming love, faith that can see everything in the light of God's governance for good, hope that can carry us through the most discouraging of circumstances, and power to overcome evil and do what is right.

I urge everyone ... to experience a private retreat at least once a year. A weekend is a wonderful time frame....

First, choose a place that is free from distraction. Go to a retreat center.... Or perhaps you can find a mountain cabin, or a beach house.

Second, stoutly refuse to over-structure the time. Long prayer-filled walks are often more useful than hectic-filled rituals. Quiet meditation on a single phrase of Scripture is frequently preferable to panting through many chapters. Reflecting in a journal on the work of God within us is usually more profitable than massive reading of devotional literature. Sometimes nothing should be done—simply and intentionally "waste" time for God.[20]

Such wilderness time in spiritual retreat is like coming home to God and resting in Him. Emilie Griffin has provided practical and helpful guidelines for how to have a one-day, three-day, and even seven-day spiritual retreat in her book *Wilderness Time*.[21] Ultimately, it is not how we plan the retreat that determines the outcome of the retreat. It is God Himself who will meet with us in ways that only *He* can orchestrate. God is the God of retreats, and we are not!

Wasting time for God in solitude and silence, including spiritual retreat, is therefore an essential means of experiencing God's rest and peace in a noisy and restless world. An essential part of solitude and silence is *contemplative prayer,* which Tricia Rhodes describes in *The Soul at Rest* as the only type of prayer that can create balance in the busyness of life and help the soul to be at rest. She writes:

> Very simply, contemplative prayer is communing with God through quiet moments of meditation, listening, and reflecting on Him. It is our response to God's call to "be still, and know."
>
> This is called the "inner prayer journey" because instead of rushing into prayer with an agenda or grocery list of requests, we quiet our souls until God can speak and we are able to hear His gentle voice. His Word breathes new life into our spiritual walk as we let *Him* write its truths on our heart. We enter into a love affair with the God of the universe.[22]

Rhodes provides helpful guidelines and suggestions for practicing meditative prayer, Scripture praying, listening prayer, recollective prayer, the prayer of detachment, prayer through the dark night, and contemplative prayer.

Similarly, Jan Johnson, in *When the Soul Listens,* shares insights on finding rest and direction in contemplative prayer.[23] Also very helpful is Dallas Willard's *Hearing God,* an updated edition of his classic book on divine guidance and developing a conversational relationship with God so that we can hear His voice.[24] Leanne Payne likewise has written an excellent book, *Listening Prayer,* on learning to hear God's voice and keep a prayer journal.[25]

Let me conclude this chapter with more wise words from Richard Foster:

> Solitude is one of the deepest disciplines of the spiritual life because it crucifies our need for importance and prominence. Everyone—including ourselves at first—will see solitude as a waste of good time. We are removed from "where the action is." That, of course, is exactly what we need. In silence and solitude God slowly but surely frees us from our egomania.
>
> In time we come to see that the really important action occurs in solitude. Once we have experienced God at work in the soul, all the blare and attention of the world seems like a distant and fragmentary echo. Only then are we able to enter the hustle and bustle of today's machine civilization with perspective and freedom.[26]

And rest—in the Lord!

The psalmist says in Psalm 91:1-2, "He who dwells in the shelter of the Most High will rest in the shadow of the Almighty. I will say of the Lord, 'He is my refuge and my fortress, my God, in whom I trust.'" In Psalm 46:10a we read, "Be still, and know that I am God." And in Psalm 27:14, "Wait for the Lord; be strong and take heart and wait for the Lord."

# Simplicity

Both Christian and secular books on simplicity, simple living, or simplifying your life abound today. This contemporary interest in simplicity may reflect the longing in many of us for a return to simple living and a less hurried and harried lifestyle. We are tired of the hustle-bustle, tired of the frantic, frenzied way of life in today's society, at least in North America. We long for simplicity: we long for rest and a more contented life.

"Though it has been commended and practiced for centuries, simplicity has seldom been more needed than it is today. Health requires it. Sanity demands it. Contentment facilitates it," writes Richard Swenson.[1] In the midst of a restless world where turmoil and trouble are more the rule than tranquility, simplicity is another essential means of entering more into God's rest and peace.

William D. Watkins writes:

How can we survive life's inevitable onslaughts? We must have a center to our lives, an eye in the midst of the storm where calm and peace reign. We must, in other words, have the discipline of simplicity.

Simplicity is an inner attitude and focus that steadies and secures us. It brings us confidence that no matter what comes against us and threatens to topple us, we can withstand. Simplicity helps us see what has eternal value and what does not, what we dare not live without and what we must let loose from our hands. When learned and practiced well, simplicity gives us the gift of peace and contentment whether life showers us with calm and plenty or harrowing storms and agonizing loss.[2]

Simplicity is therefore a spiritual discipline that enables us to stay in the calm eye of the storm, to remain Shepherd-centered in Christ. Simplicity can be more specifically described as "practicing a lifestyle free of excess, greed, and covetousness so that we can draw closer to God and reach out to others in compassionate service. As we enter into simplicity, the Holy Spirit empowers us to seek first the kingdom of God, to keep our eyes on Jesus, and to live free of crippling anxiety and lust for money."[3]

Contentment in whatever circumstances (see Heb 13:5; Phil 4:11-13) and generosity in giving away our money and possessions (see 2 Cor 8:9; 9:6-15) are crucial aspects of simplicity. Simplicity, with contentment and generosity, therefore enables us, by the power of the Holy Spirit, to overcome our sinful tendency toward greed and covetousness, especially the lust for or love of money, which the Bible states "is a root of all kinds of evil" (1 Tm 6:10). We are actually warned in Scripture not to fall into the trap of greedy accumulation of more and more possessions or riches (for example, see Ps 62:10; Prv 11:28; Lk 12:15; 1 Tm 6:9-10). In fact, Jesus says emphatically and clearly in Matthew 6:24, "No one can serve two masters. Either he will hate the one and love the other, or he will be devoted to the one and despise the other. You cannot serve both God and Money."

Practicing simplicity in the power of the Spirit is a means of overcoming such greed or love of money and things, thereby freeing us to live in peace and God's rest. For some of us, the Holy Spirit may give particular spiritual gifts that will greatly enhance our ability to practice simplicity: spiritual gifts such as giving (Rom 12:8), mercy (Rom 12:8), hospitality (1 Pt 4:9), and voluntary poverty (1 Cor 13:1-3).[4] I will never forget a slogan that I read on a friend's briefcase years ago: "I live simply that others may simply live!"

Richard Foster has authored an excellent book called *Freedom of Simplicity*. Simplicity does indeed lead to freedom to live the abundant and eternal life we have received in Christ. Foster describes three major types of simplicity: *inward simplicity*, which is focused on the divine center within our hearts and on holy obedience; *outward simplicity*, with gradual steps toward living a simpler lifestyle characterized by giving, service, and sacrifice, and to unclutter our lives of unnecessary things or possessions and identify with the poor; and *corporate simplicity*, which has to do with the church, as well as with the world at large, including dealing with difficult issues of economics, world hunger, and international trade.[5]

### Inward Simplicity

Simplicity must begin with our heart in inward simplicity. Inward simplicity is a matter of the heart in which we focus on the divine center, the Lord Himself, who dwells within us by the

Holy Spirit. In this singular focus on Him, we seek His kingdom first (Mt 6:33), surrendering every area of our lives to His lordship in holy obedience.

Thomas Kelly has described beautifully such an inner simplicity focused on the divine center in his classic book, *A Testament of Devotion:*

> Life is meant to be lived from a Center, a divine Center. Each one of us can live such a life of amazing power and peace and serenity, of integration and confidence and simplified multiplicity, on one condition—that is, *if we really want to.* There is a divine Abyss within us all, a holy Infinite Center, a Heart, a Life who speaks in us and through us to the world.
>
> Our real problem, in failing to center down, is not a lack of time; it is, I fear, in too many of us, lack of joyful, enthusiastic delight in Him, lack of deep, deep-drawing love directed toward Him at every hour of the day and night ... and I find He never guides us into an intolerable scramble of panting feverishness. The Cosmic Patience becomes, in part, our patience, for after all God is at work in the world....
>
> Life from the Center is a life of unhurried peace and power. It is simple. It is serene. It is amazing. It is triumphant. It is radiant.... We need not get frantic. He is at the helm. And when our little day is done we lie down quietly in peace, for all is well.[6]

As we live in the divine center of God's presence and God's will, we will experience the deep rest and peace of God, with freedom from crippling anxiety. Foster has noted that three inner attitudes are characteristic of such freedom from anxiety: "If what we have we receive as a gift, and if what we have is to be cared for by God, and if what we have is available to others, then we will possess freedom from anxiety. *This is the inward reality of simplicity.*⁷

Elisabeth Elliot, whose first husband was the martyred missionary Jim Elliot, has written about her own experience of keeping a quiet heart, similar to living in the divine center:

One rainy afternoon at Wheaton College in 1947, my friend Sarah Spiro and I were at the piano in Williston Hall. I had written down a few lines of a prayer....

> Lord, give to me a quiet heart
> That does not ask to understand
> But confident steps forward in
> The darkness guided by Thy hand.

This was my heart's desire then. It is the same today. A willing acceptance of all that God assigns and a glad surrender of all that I am and have constitute the key to receiving the gift of a quiet heart. Whenever I have balked, the quietness goes. It is restored and life immeasurably simplified, when I have trusted and obeyed.

God loves us with an everlasting love. He is unutterably merciful and kind, and sees to it that not a day passes without the opportunity for new applications of the old truth of *becoming* a child of God. This, to me, sums up the meaning of life.[8]

Jeremiah Burroughs (1599–1646) was well known as a leading English Puritan preacher of his time. He wrote a classic book called *The Rare Jewel of Christian Contentment,* first published posthumously in 1648. His definition of Christian contentment comes close to living life in the divine center, with simplicity and rest in the Lord: "Christian contentment is that sweet, inward, quiet, gracious frame of spirit, which freely submits to and delights in God's wise and fatherly disposal in every condition."[9] Though the language is dated, this definition of Christian contentment is beautiful and it captures the single-hearted focus of inward simplicity. Burroughs concluded, "Oh, the Word holds forth a way full of comfort and peace to the people of God even in this world. You may live happy lives in the midst of all the storms and tempests in the world. There is an ark that you may come into, and no men in the world may live such comfortable, cheerful and contented lives as the saints of God."[10]

The singleness of heart and mind with a focus on the Lord that is a crucial characteristic of inward simplicity can be found in a few Scripture texts on the theme of "one thing." For example, David in Psalm 27:4 says, "One thing I ask of the Lord, this is what I seek: that I may dwell in the house of the Lord all the days of my life, to gaze upon the beauty of the Lord and to seek him in the temple." A second example is found in Luke 10:38-42 in the well-known story about Jesus visiting Martha and Mary at Martha's home. Martha was very busy with preparations that were needed to entertain or serve her special guest, Jesus. Mary was sitting instead at the Lord's feet, listening to what He said. When Martha complained to Jesus that Mary was not helping her, this was part of His reply: "but only one thing is needed. Mary has chosen what is better, and it will not be taken away from her" (v. 42).

One more example of the focus on "one thing" can be found in the life of the apostle Paul. He says clearly in Philippians 3:13b-14: "But one thing I do: Forgetting what is behind and straining toward what is ahead, I press on toward the goal to win the prize for which God has called me heavenward in Christ Jesus."

In inward simplicity, we focus on *one thing:* living in the divine center, seeking Him and His kingdom first in holy obedience.

## The Many Facets of Simplicity

Kim Thomas, in a recent book, *Simplicity,* on finding peace by uncluttering your life, suggested a biblically based three-part process for practicing simplicity: reducing the clutter, persevering in the everyday, and focusing on the goal. She writes about simplicity in three areas: BODY (Simplicity in Our Physical World), SOUL (Simplicity in Our Relational/Emotional World), and SPIRIT (Simplicity in Our Spiritual World).[11]

In a similar vein, H. Norman Wright also recently wrote a book, *Simplify Your Life and Get More Out of It!* He has some helpful suggestions about simplifying our lives in several different areas: simplifying our pace (dealing with time management and hurry illness), simplifying our expectations (measuring success biblically and living with balanced priorities), simplifying our activities (dealing with being overloaded and driven, and energy drainers and energy boosters), simplifying our possessions (downscaling our things and living on less), simplifying our relationships (dealing with the people who clutter our lives and dumping excess emotional baggage), and simplifying our spiritual lives (doing the best thing and letting our souls catch up to our bodies). He also has a concluding chapter on helping you set up a personal plan for simplifying your life in all these areas.[12]

In order to simplify or uncomplicate your life, Philip

Patterson and Michael Herndon have described four methods to help you prioritize your life so that you can begin to differentiate the trivial from the important:

1. *The deathbed priority test....* Louise Lague suggests asking yourself, "On your deathbed, will you wish you'd spent more prime weekend hours grocery shopping or walking in the woods with your kids?" The same goes for overtime, promotions that bring more responsibilities, and even volunteer work.
2. *The disaster test....* "If an earthquake, fire, flood or other natural disaster were to strike your life tomorrow, could you get by without the item in question?"
3. *The what-if-this-didn't-exist test....* Ask yourself: "What is the worst thing that could happen if this piece of paper didn't exist?" If the answer is "nothing" ... [toss] it.
4. *The time dollars test....* Begin thinking of everything you want in terms of the amount of time it will take, after taxes and other deductions, to have enough money to buy that item. Then ask yourself, "What else could I have done with that amount of time? Which is the better use of my time?"[13]

Finally, Doug Gregg and I have provided several basic guidelines for the practice of what we have called "everyday simplicity." Buy things to meet your basic needs; turn away from things that have a hold on you; focus on enjoying the things available to you that you do not own; let your thoughts, speech, and actions be simple and straightforward—Jesus has taught us to let our "Yes" be "Yes" and our "No" be "No" (Mt 5:37), nothing more, nothing less, and nothing else; look for the Holy Spirit to be at work in the so-called interruptions of your life—

they may turn out to be divine appointments; and turn away from anything that seeks to take the place of God as our first love.[14]

Everyday simplicity can be practiced because we have come to realize, in belief as well as in experience, the reality of God's goodness and providence. He will take care of us and provide whatever we need, not necessarily whatever we want. Jesus taught this truth very clearly in Matthew 6:31-34, where He says to us,

> So do not worry, saying, "What shall we eat?" or "What shall we drink?" or "What shall we wear?" For the pagans run after all these things, and your heavenly Father knows that you need them. But seek first his kingdom and his righteousness, and all these things will be given to you as well. Therefore do not worry about tomorrow, for tomorrow will worry about itself. Each day has enough trouble of its own.

Dallas Willard, in his excellent book *The Divine Conspiracy*, has this amazing thing to say, based on Matthew 6: "With this magnificent God positioned among us, Jesus brings the assurance that our universe is *a perfectly safe place for us to be.*"[15] This does not mean that we cannot be hurt or injured physically, emotionally, spiritually, or relationally (socially). But it does mean that God will take care of us and provide for us, with grace always sufficient for our every need (2 Cor 12:9), so that in the long run, we will not be harmed forever. We are ultimately and eternally safe in the Lord, even on earth and in this universe now. And certainly in eternity, in heaven to come.

We are "safe in God's love" in this universe, as John Ortberg has put it. In asking the question, "What would my life look like

if I lived in the settled conviction that because of God's character and competence this world is a perfectly safe place for me to
be?" Ortberg offers the following answers: My anxiety level
would go down; I would be an unhurried person; I would not
be defeated by guilt; and I would trust God enough to risk
obeying him.... A person in whom the peace of Christ reigns
would be an oasis of sanity in a world of pandemonium.... A
community in which the peace of Christ reigns would change
the world."[16]

### The Practice of Simplicity: Concrete Steps

There are many practical, concrete suggestions that have been
made for the actual practice of simplicity, of what Foster has
called outward and corporate simplicity. In listing some of these
suggestions, I am not trying to overwhelm you but simply to
give you an idea of what a simple lifestyle can look like. We all
have different personalities, and some of these suggestions will
work better for some of us than others. This is also true for
other spiritual disciplines, such as solitude and silence and
prayer.[17] Some of us will pray and be silent in solitude for long
periods of time and enjoy it. Others will pray for shorter periods
each time and will pray short, even "flash prayers," at different
times during the day. Likewise, let the Lord guide you by His
Spirit about which of these concrete ways of practicing everyday
simplicity in our lives may apply to you. Leave alone those that
may not be relevant to you. And start simply! The simplicity of
simplicity must overcome the complexity of simplicity! I am
aware of the danger of being legalistic in slavishly following lists
for practicing simplicity concretely. Again, pray for the Holy

Spirit's guidance and obey Him, not the lists per se.

I will share with you two long lists of concrete steps for practicing simplicity and living a simpler lifestyle. The first is taken from a book called *Spiritual Simplicity*, written by David Yount. Here are some of his practical steps to simplify your life:

A. STEPS TO SAVE TIME AND REDUCE STRESS: Get rid of things you don't use. Do laundry just once a week. Keep out-of-doors chores to a minimum. Don't run unnecessary errands. Stop junk mail. Clear the paper clutter. Let your answering machine take your phone calls. Keep holy the Sabbath Day. Turn waiting time into meditating time. Stamp out deadbeat relationships. Don't lose sleep. Keep a journal. Say "no" or "not now."

B. STEPS TO SAVE (AND EVEN MAKE) MONEY: Buy a used car. Establish a spending plan. Pay off credit card balances promptly. Use your checking account for regular bills only. Consider moving into a more economical home. Let the taxpayers pay for your children's education. Use discount phone service and e-mail. Borrow or rent rather than buy. Take lunches to work and school. Get out of debt. Pay off your mortgage.

C. STEPS TO SAVE BOTH TIME AND MONEY: Shop only once a week and buy in bulk. Simplify your wardrobe. Buy ahead for holidays, birthdays, and anniversaries. Don't wait to get sick before seeing the doctor. Entertain at home. Travel simply. Prepare for tax time. Shop for the lowest cost insurance.[18]

Yount's list is a general list of concrete steps you can take for simplifying your life. In a more specifically Christian context, K.P. Yohannan in a challenging book, *The Road to Reality*, provides us with a second list of over fifty items that he came up with after brainstorming with a few friends on how to simplify our lives and save money for world evangelism, or practice what he calls "New Testament Simplicity." I will list only a few of his suggestions in the eight categories he covered:

### Shoppers
Avoid designer labels. Pay cash and don't use credit cards. Buy at thrift stores or warehouse/outlets. Buy used cars and major appliances.

### Parents
Organize a babysitting co-op. Organize car pools. Be moderate in giving toys to children. Become more involved in free outdoor activities.

### Housekeepers
Make a budget ... and stick to it. Cut down on use of electricity and other utilities. Use reusable plastic food containers rather than plastic wraps and foil to store leftovers.

### Employees
Bring your lunch to work. Buddy up and share professional resources.

### Ladies
Reduce use of cosmetics and beauty products. Avoid seasonal fashion buying.

### Men
Wait for sales to buy suits and shoes. Don't purchase rarely used sporting goods. Carefully evaluate the real need for expensive power tools and elaborate stereo systems.

### Everyone
Cut down on magazine and catalog subscriptions. Evaluate and reduce cost and length of vacations. Reduce costly entertainment.

## Clergy

Reconsider and simplify use of ecclesiastical furnishings. Reduce the size of your library, and don't buy books you will use only once. Reevaluate the entire church budget every year to channel funds away from selfish uses and toward missions.[19]

Yohannan is serious and hard-hitting about following Jesus all the way, including simplifying our lives, especially for the sake of spreading the gospel. He does stress, however, that the concrete ideas he has suggested may or may not apply in your particular life situation. We are called to simplify our lifestyle and practice everyday simplicity according to the Holy Spirit's leading and not fall into legalism.

I must confess that Yohannan's idea for clergy to reduce the size of their library and not buy books they will use only once struck me particularly hard. I am both a senior pastor of a local church and a professor of psychology at Fuller Theological Seminary. As a pastor and scholar, I am into books a lot, literally and figuratively! My libraries at home, at Fuller, and at church have continued to grow as I add more and more books that I feel I need for my research and ministry, for writing and sermon preparation.

In fact, while I was writing this chapter on simplicity on the day after Thanksgiving, there was a special After Thanksgiving Day Sale at a local bookstore in Pasadena, not far from where I live in neighboring Arcadia. I had to pray and really resist the temptation to go to the book sale. I succeeded with the Lord's help and stayed home all day and almost finished writing this chapter. I had practiced simplicity and felt good about not buying more books! My wife Angela was especially thrilled at this, because she often laments over how much space my books take up, especially at home. However, the next day I had to go to this bookstore to pick up a book I needed for my research and reading as I prepared myself to start writing the next chapter of this book on the Sabbath. I need to confess that I ended up buying several other books, although most of them were related to the topic of rest!

I am keenly aware of how I can easily rationalize my book buying because I need the books in my work as a scholar and pastor. Reducing my library will be near to impossible for now, but I hear the Lord speaking to me about *not* buying books that I really don't need. I often respond by telling myself I am buying those books so that my other pastoral staff and colleagues can have access to them: I freely loan them out! But simplicity that leads to God's peace and rest and contentment means that I need to ask for the Holy Spirit's control over this area of my life. Come to think of it, Angela's repeated suggestion that I give away or donate books that I don't need now is an excellent one. Perhaps I can "reduce" the size of my library in this sense after all. I have less of a struggle in other areas, such as buying my clothes and suits on sale, giving money and other resources to help the poor and needy, and advancing God's kingdom through missions and church ministries.

Let me end this chapter by relating an incident that happened in my home recently. Angela and I both work. She is a C.P.A. and controller of a fresh produce company in downtown L.A. Our children are both in school: Andrew is in high school, and Carolyn is in college at U.C.L.A. Every Monday we have a cleaning lady who comes into our home and does the cleaning for the whole day. Several weeks ago, she accidentally damaged an expensive cuckoo clock that Angela and I had bought in

Germany while we were on a family vacation with our children. We were both very upset at this and angrily reprimanded her for her terrible mistake. I almost immediately realized how attached I still can be to the things of this world. After all, it is only a cuckoo clock! I confessed my sin to the Lord and more calmly talked to the cleaning lady about the whole incident. My initial angry response and lack of simplicity needed repentance on my part.

Living in the divine center is possible, but we can so easily slip out of that centeredness in Christ. Simplicity helps us to stay there in and with Him. But simplicity is not a one-shot deal. It is a process. We need to grow in simplicity, and as the Holy Spirit helps us, we will grow deeper into the heart of God and His peace and rest. And a big part of entering God's rest has to do with keeping the Sabbath, the topic of the next chapter.

*Seven*

❧

# Sabbath

M any Christians, when asked what the Sabbath means to them, will probably answer with a text like Mark 2:27, quoting Jesus, "The sabbath was made for humankind, and not humankind for the sabbath" (NRSV). The common conclusion, therefore, is that there is now no need for any legalistic observance of the Sabbath: a twenty-four-hour day once a week of ceasing from work, resting and worshiping God, thereby keeping it holy, is not a law we need to follow today.

While we may acknowledge that it is a good idea to take periodic "Sabbaths" to rest, we feel it doesn't have to be once a week for a twenty-four-hour day as the Jewish people have always understood the Sabbath to mean. This common conclusion is dangerous, however, because it is not completely correct. God gave us the Sabbath to benefit or bless us, and it is to our own detriment that we ignore one of His Ten Commandments, given in Exodus 20:8-11:

> Remember the Sabbath day by keeping it holy, six days you shall labor and do all your work, but the seventh day is a

Sabbath to the Lord your God. On it you shall not do any work.... For in six days the Lord made the heavens and the earth, the sea, and all that is in them, but He rested on the seventh day. Therefore the Lord blessed the Sabbath day and made it holy.

Also, in Deuteronomy 5:15, we read, "Remember that you were slaves in Egypt and that the Lord your God brought you out of there with a mighty hand and an outstretched arm. Therefore the Lord your God has commanded you to observe the Sabbath day."

God did not suggest keeping the Sabbath—He commanded it! We, therefore, need to take another look, a closer and more accurate one, at the Sabbath and how it really is part of God's infinitely wise way of helping us to enter more fully into His rest. But first, let us see how even the world at large has begun to acknowledge that Sabbath keeping (or taking a day off to rest from work every week) may be a good practice to follow.

## Sabbath: A Good Practice

The idea of taking off one day a week to rest from the usual hustle-and-bustle of our lives—Sabbath keeping—has recently received some good press. For example, Leonard Felder, a licensed psychologist in private practice in West Los Angeles, has written a book, *The Ten Challenges,* in which he draws out spiritual lessons from the Ten Commandments for creating meaning, growth, and richness every day of your life. In describing the "fourth challenge," or fourth commandment of remembering the Sabbath day to keep it holy, he writes:

Imagine for a moment that someone who cares about you has sent you a gift certificate for a day that is to be devoted entirely to the needs of your soul. On that day you don't have to work. You can take a walk and have a relaxing conversation with friends or loved ones about the things that really matter. You can meditate, pray, and read the books that speak to your soul. You can nap and let your mind take a rest, or dance and sing to let your spirit soar. For one day, you can stop trying to prove yourself out in the world. You can look at your life as a blessing and feel at peace with where you are right now. Instead of feeling fragmented and pressured, you can spend the day in a generous, positive, and contemplative mood.

Does this sound too good to be true? You may be surprised to discover that this gift certificate ... is actually the fourth commandment.[1]

Borrowing mainly from Jewish and Christian sources (but also using other religious traditions), Felder suggests four steps for deepening your sense of freedom each week as you use the "gift certificate" of observing the Sabbath day:

1. Decide what you need to stop doing each Sabbath so that you can enjoy a day of freedom from the strivings of the material world;

2. Choose a few favorite activities that will give you a sense of Sabbath joy, for example, lighting candles, napping, making love with your spouse, walking, preparing and enjoying a special meal with family or friends, singing, dancing, praying blessings for family members, doing spiritual study, giving to charity, and having special conversations with gratitude;

3. Use the blessings and prayers of the Sabbath as a means of opening up your own heart; and

4. Try to take as much of the Sabbath feeling as possible with you into the rest of the week.[2]

In a similar vein, the well-known author Laura Schlessinger, together with Rabbi Stewart Vogel, recently coauthored *The Ten Commandments*, in which they describe the significance of God's laws in everyday life. With reference to the fourth commandment, they emphasized, "The Sabbath is *not* about time off; it is about sacred time."[3] In each sacred or holy time, they suggested the following: not working for financial reward or competing for awards, making time to relax and do nothing, reading and studying religious materials, taking leisurely walks, enjoying wonderful meals and discussions with friends and neighbors, talking with children, attending religious services, praying and contemplating, and lovemaking with your spouse.[4]

In an interesting book only indirectly related to the Sabbath and its emphasis on ceasing from work and resting, David Kundtz, another psychotherapist in private practice, wrote about *Stopping*, on how to be still when you have to keep going. He defined "stopping" as follows: "Stopping is doing nothing as much as possible, for a definite period of time (one second to one month) for the purpose of becoming more fully awake and remembering who you are."[5] He also identified and described three levels or ways of stopping based on the duration of time involved: Stillpoints, Stopovers, and Grinding Halts.

A Stillpoint is stopping quickly and doing nothing for just a moment ... a few seconds to a few minutes.... Somewhat less frequent are Stopovers, which are those times that are longer than a Stillpoint, an hour to several days.... A Grinding Halt will probably happen only a couple of times in most people's lives. They are times from a week to a month, or more, and typically happen at times of life transitions.[6]

Kundtz also points out that slowing down and Stopping are not the same thing: "Stopping is not slowing down ... even though an important aspect of Stopping ... is, in fact, to slow down. The process of Stopping is very different from the process of slowing down. Trying to slow down does not slow you down ... slowing down doesn't work because everything around us is going so fast."[7]

Although Kundtz includes a day off for rest and rejuvenation as an example of a Stopover,[8] he does not deal explicitly with Sabbath keeping. His idea of Stopping, however, comes close to the ceasing from work and resting aspects of the Sabbath. Keeping the Sabbath, of course, has deeper spiritual and religious significance, especially that of worshiping God, but I will cover this crucial aspect of Sabbath rest later in this chapter. For now, Stopping can be viewed as a more general, perhaps more secular version of the idea of Sabbath. The world at large longs to stop, or at least pause periodically. The need for Sabbath is even more obvious in today's rushed and restless world. We do need to stop—and Sabbath, or keep the Sabbath!

Wayne Muller, an ordained minister and therapist who founded Bread for the Journey, an organization serving families in need, wrote a whole book on the Sabbath entitled *Sabbath: Restoring the Sacred Rhythm of Rest*. Muller pulls together ideas and practices related to rest and the Sabbath from different religious traditions, including not only Jewish and Christian sources but also others, such as Buddhist ones. He begins by emphatically denouncing the violence of our current lifestyles accelerating ever more to achieve so-called success. He writes:

> A "successful" life has become a violent enterprise. We make war on our bodies, pushing them beyond their limits; war on our children because we cannot find enough time to be with them when they are hurt or afraid, and need our company; war on our spirit, because we are too preoccupied to listen to the quiet voices that seek to nourish and refresh us; war on our communities, because we are fearfully protecting what we have…; war on the earth, because we cannot take the time to place our feet on the ground and allow it to feed us.[9]

Muller quotes Thomas Merton's powerful and challenging words, which we do well to heed again today:

> There is a pervasive form of contemporary violence … [and that is] activism and overwork.… To allow oneself to be carried away by a multitude of conflicting concerns, to surrender to too many demands, to commit oneself to too many projects, to want to help everyone in everything, is to succumb to violence.[10]

The answer to overcoming our contemporary tendency to such violence in our lives is to heed the sacred rhythm of rest that is in the keeping of the Sabbath. Muller reminds us that Sabbath keeping is a commandment from God, not a lifestyle suggestion! It is as important as not stealing, not lying, not murdering. Therefore, "Remember to rest."[11]

While he does include the Sabbath as referring to a single day each week, Muller takes the view that Sabbath time can also be a Sabbath hour, a Sabbath afternoon, or even a Sabbath walk.

Americans now consume double the amount of goods and services per person compared to 1945. The "Gospel of Mass Consumption" is Muller's terminology for the vision of progress that has consumed us![12] He therefore states, "Sabbath is a time to stop, to refrain from being seduced by our desires. To stop working, stop making money, stop spending money … just stop."[13] It is interesting to note that Muller independently uses the language of *Stopping!* He also describes how we can be Sabbath for one another, emphasizing the social or relational aspect of rest: "At our best, we become Sabbath for one another. We are the emptiness, the day of rest. We become space, that our loved ones, the lost and sorrowful, may find rest in us."[14]

Finally, in his suggestions for what we can do on a Sabbath day, he provides a list based on what ancient texts say, similar to what has already been mentioned earlier in this chapter: lighting candles, singing songs, praying, telling stories, worshiping, eating, napping, and making love.[15]

## The Jewish Sabbath

Although the Sabbath has been viewed recently as a good idea and practice for the health and well-being of overworked and stressed-out Americans desperately in need of some rest and peace, it is certainly more than just a good thing for our health and welfare! We need to have a better understanding of the original context and meaning of the fourth commandment, of the Jewish Sabbath, in order to better appreciate the Sabbath as a means of experiencing God's rest. While the books that I have already reviewed and referred to in this chapter have made use of Jewish writings and sources for Sabbath keeping, let me briefly highlight the main aspects of the original Jewish Sabbath, given by God as the fourth commandment for the Jews to observe and keep holy.

The late Paul K. Jewett, who was a professor of Systematic Theology at Fuller Theological Seminary for many years, wrote a comprehensive and excellent theological guide to the Lord's Day, or the Christian day of worship (Sunday) in which he also provided a good overview of the Jewish Sabbath. The Sabbath has been a crucial and significant part of Jewish history, and its importance cannot be overemphasized. In fact, Jewett wrote, "The Sabbath was to be kept inviolate as the weightiest part of the law. It became virtually synonymous to say Yahweh gave Israel the law and to say Yahweh commanded her to keep holy the Sabbath."[16]

Jewish essayist Achad Haam has been quoted as saying, "We can affirm without any exaggeration that the Sabbath has preserved the Jews more than the Jews have preserved the Sabbath."[17]

Karen Burton Mains and her husband David Mains, both well-known Christian leaders and authors, had a life-changing experience when they went to Israel in the fall of 1977. They were particularly touched by how seriously, yet joyously, the Jewish people practiced Sabbath keeping. As a result, Karen Mains has written a very helpful book, *Making Sunday Special.* She noted that her husband researched the Jewish Sabbath after they returned from their ten-day trip to Israel. He found that a devout Jew would spend three days anticipating, or looking forward to, the Sabbath (Friday evening at sundown to Saturday evening at sundown) and three days after the Sabbath to reflect on it because the Sabbath was so special and sacred.[18]

Karen Mains also provided a very practical description of Jewish Sabbath tradition. Here is her overview of what happens on a Jewish Sabbath:

1. First there is the lighting of the candles which is traditionally done by the wife, mother, or woman of the house—two candles symbolizing the words, *observe* [Deuteronomy 5:12] and *remember* [Exodus 20:8]....

2. The Kabalat Shabbat is an ancient prayer service made of introductory psalms and the psalm for the Sabbath Day. The evening service follows including the central reference to the creation theme....

3. The blessing of the children....

4. The family sings "Peace Be unto You"—a welcome to the angels....

5. The husband blesses his wife using ... Proverbs 31:10-31....

6. The wine is blessed using the Kiddush—a prayer of sanctification for the Sabbath.

7. There is a ritual hand-washing and then the blessing over the challot, the traditional braided bread.

8. The meal is eaten and *enjoyed* with singing and much laughter.

9. A grace is said when the meal is ended, an official closure based on Deuteronomy 8:10....

10. The rest of the evening before bedtime is usually spent talking to family and friends and/or in the study of the Torah.[19]

These are the major customs related to the Friday Shabbat meal practiced by devout Jews.

Another ritual that devout Jews engage in at the end of the Sabbath when it is dark enough on Saturday evening is the

Havdalah service. A special braided candle is lighted, with a prayer of blessing over wine and spices, and then the Havdalah prayers are recited. This service is done at home or in a group context. A special moment comes in the service when a blessing is said to thank God for the spices of life. Then a small spice box is shaken, and a deep breath of its fragrance is inhaled one last time, with a quiet vow to carry the feeling or vision of the Sabbath into the next six days of the week before another Sabbath arrives![20]

## The Lord's Day: Sabbath for Christians

Most Christians now celebrate and observe the Sabbath on Sunday or the Lord's Day, the first day of the week, rather than on Saturday, or the seventh day of the week. Jewett has provided some helpful historical and theological reasons for this practice. He writes:

> We venture that the physical rest of the Old Testament Sabbath has been reinterpreted in the New Testament as having its fulfillment in Christ, who delivers the Christian from the bondage of sin (Calvin). But since this fulfillment is in principle, not in finality, there must be continuity, though not identity, between the physical rest of the Jewish Sabbath and the rest of the Lord's Day.... We would like to suggest the following four general principles ... in keeping the Lord's Day:
>
> 1. He rightly observes the day ... who does so in a faith which renounces all confidence in himself and his own works and rests in God only for deliverance from the guilt

and power of sin…. Thus the Lord's Day rest is preeminently a soul rest, a spiritual experience….

2. He rightly observes the day … who meets with God's people on this day….

3. He rightly observes the day … who does so with joy…. "The Lord is risen; he is risen indeed."

4. He rightly observes the day … who acknowledges that it especially belongs to the Lord. It is he who has hallowed and sanctified the day.[21]

In more concrete terms, Karen Mains suggests the following steps that we can take as Christians to observe and remember our Sabbath or Sunday, the Lord's Day, starting with Saturday evening:

1. The lighting of candles
2. The blessing over the meal
3. The meal with specially planned table conversation
4. The blessing of the children and spouses
5. The God Hunt for children
6. The God Hunt for adults (with younger children allowed to play with special toys from the Sabbath basket)
7. A prayer in preparation for Sunday

The "God Hunt" refers to any time or occasion God intervenes in our lives and we recognize it is He, such as an obvious answer to prayer.[22] In the rest of her book, Mains provides other helpful suggestions for preparing physically, emotionally, and spiritually for the Lord's Day, and also for how to make Sunday itself special! She enthusiastically reminds us, "God gives us fifty-two Sabbaths, or seven and a half weeks of vacation time per year!—

time during which we are to do no work. As Thomas Aquinas put it, each week one goes on *ad vacandum divinis*—a day of vacation with God."[23]

For those of us who are ministers or who serve on a church staff, Sundays may be our busiest day of the week! We may therefore have to choose another day of the week other than Sunday as a Sabbath, to keep it holy. As David Seamands puts it, "The Sabbath is ... a gracious gift to recreate body and soul. Let us not profane this gift. Let us keep it a holy day, even though others all around us may turn it into a holiday. Let us make it a day of rest and worship and joy."[24]

David Ford, Regius Professor of Divinity at Cambridge University in England, has pointed out that the guiding principle underlying Sabbaths, feasts, and fasts is simple: "We are created first to enjoy God and creation at leisure, and unless special times are devoted to this, we will be trapped in unhealthy compulsions and idolatries."[25]

As we aim to keep the Sabbath in a Christian sense (not legalistically, because the Lord Jesus did say in Mark 2:27-28 that the Sabbath was made for humankind and not humankind for the Sabbath), we still need to keep the Sabbath wholly. Marva Dawn has written an excellent book on how we as Christians can practice keeping the Sabbath wholly, by ceasing, resting, embracing, and feasting. Her chapter titles are provocative and insightful. With regard to ceasing, she has ceasing work; ceasing productivity and accomplishment; ceasing anxiety, worry, and tension; ceasing our trying to be God; ceasing our possessiveness; ceasing our enculturation; ceasing the humdrum and meaninglessness. With regard to resting, she writes about spiritual rest, physical rest, emotional rest, intellectual rest, social rest, aids to rest, and an ethics of character. With regard to embracing, she includes embracing intentionality, embracing the values of the Christian community, embracing time rather than space, embracing giving instead of requiring, embracing our calling in life, embracing wholeness or *shalom*, and embracing the world. Finally, with regard to feasting, she describes feasting on the eternal, feasting with music, feasting with beauty, feasting with food, feasting with affection, and feasting and festival.[26]

Dawn writes, "In our American culture, in which every person is judged by his or her work, and rest is determined by our labors, we desperately need this radical reorientation made possible by the Jewish concept of time in which rest determines our work."[27] As Abraham Heschel has put it,

> The Sabbath as a day of rest, as a day of abstaining from toil, is not for the purpose of recovering one's lost strength and becoming fit for the forthcoming labor. The Sabbath is a day for the sake of life. Man is not a beast of burden, and the Sabbath is not for the purpose of enhancing the efficiency of his work.... The Sabbath is not for the sake of weekdays; the weekdays are for the sake of the Sabbath. It is not an interlude but the climax of living.[28]

Dawn also points out that in faithfully keeping the Sabbath each week, God enables us to know His presence even in the dark nights of our soul when He seems to be distant or even absent.[29] She emphasizes, however, that Sabbath keeping should be a joyous time of delight, as we rest, remember, and especially, worship God.

> Sabbath-keeping frees us to take delight in everything, to uncork our own spontaneity. Because there is nothing we

*have* to do, we are free suddenly to say yes to invitations, to read fairy tales, to be children, to discover the presence of God hidden all around us. To keep the Sabbath invites us to have festival fun, to play, to enjoy our guests and our activities, to relish the opportunity for worship, to celebrate the eternal presence of God himself. We feast in every aspect of our being—physical, intellectual, social, emotional, spiritual—and we feast with music, beauty, food and affection. Our bodies, minds, souls, and spirits celebrate together with others that God is in our midst.[30]

Dawn keeps her Sabbath on Sunday "because it combines the festival of the Resurrection with the tradition of the day set apart to imitate the Creator in his resting."[31]

While I agree with several authors that we can have Sabbath times that are shorter (for example, an afternoon) or longer (for example, a whole weekend retreat) than the twenty-four-hour day that is the Jewish Sabbath, I believe it is crucial for us today, even as Christians, to return to Sabbath keeping the way Dawn has beautifully described it: one day a week set aside to rest and worship God. She starts on Saturday night, by putting away all her books and work as a theologian and author, and keeps her Sabbath till Sunday night, as much as possible each week. Sunday worship at a church service is a crucial part of her Sabbath, although traveling can sometimes affect the usual Sabbath rhythm or schedule.

The Sabbath is a special day once a week that God has commanded us to observe and keep so that we can experience more fully and deeply his rest and peace. We can do this on the Lord's Day or Sunday, starting on Saturday evening until Sunday evening. Others may try around midnight Saturday to around midnight Sunday. Some of us may have to choose a different day because of work schedules (for example, pastors) or shift work (for example, nurses) that may involve a Sunday. There is no need or place for legalistic enslavement to Sabbath keeping. However, keeping the Sabbath holy and wholly is definitely still part of God's wise ways of enabling us to enter more into His rest even in this present life, albeit imperfectly for now. True Sabbath keeping and true Sabbath rest must be centered in God. Prayer is therefore crucial.

## Sabbath Prayer

I want to end this chapter by referring to what Richard Foster has called "Sabbath Prayer" as an example of the Prayer of Rest. In his excellent book *Prayer: Finding the Heart's True Home,* he described an experience he had while resting on a tiny island off the Pacific coast of Canada. He had prayed, "Refresh me, Lord. Refresh me." He sensed the Lord wanted to teach him Sabbath Prayer, and he was willing to learn. As he waited upon the Lord, he heard the words, "Be still ... rest ... *shalom.*" He heard these same words a couple more times and experienced the Lord's presence and a wonderful quiet attentiveness and calm spirit.[32] Concerning the Prayer of Rest, Foster writes:

> Through the Prayer of Rest, God places his children in the eye of the storm. When all around us is chaos and confusion, deep within we know stability and serenity. In the midst of intense personal struggle, we are still and relaxed. While a thousand frustrations seek to distract us, we remain focused and attentive. This is the fruit of the Prayer of Rest.[33]

He suggests the following prayer:

Blessed Savior, I am not good at resting in the hollow of your hand. Nothing in my experience has taught me this resting. I have been taught how to take charge. I have been taught how to be in control. But how to rest? No, I have no models, no paradigms for resting. This is not exactly right.... Manifold demands were placed upon you, and still you worked in unhurried peace and power. Help me to walk in your steps. Teach me to see only what you see, to say only what you say, to do only what you do. Help me, Lord, to work resting and pray resting. I ask this in your good and strong name. Amen.[34]

Sabbath prayer and the prayer of rest can be part of our Sabbath keeping. So can taking naps or sleep. Sleep is another crucial means of experiencing God's rest and peace, the topic of the next chapter.

# Eight

# Sleep

D o you ever have time to sleep?" I am often asked this question by people who don't know me well but are aware of my speaking schedule and my professional work as a professor and a pastor. While I do have a busy schedule, I have tried, with God's help and grace, to allow myself time to experience His rest and peace, including sleep. When I tell people that I try to get at least seven hours of sleep a night, they usually are surprised, if not shocked! I guess they expect me to say that I have little time for sleep. In fact, I know of busy business executives, as well as busy pastors, who sleep only four to five hours each night. Unfortunately, many who have to cope with the frenetic pace of life in the twenty-first century do not value sleep very much.

When I was speaking at a conference for pastors and church leaders a number of years ago in Asia, I asked the key pastors present how much sleep they were getting each night, on the average. Almost all of them indicated they were having only four hours of sleep a night. One of them was so convicted of his need for more sleep during my talk that he took the afternoon off and went home for a long nap! He came up to me later to apologize for skipping the afternoon session. I quickly told him there was no need to apologize. In fact, I said I was really glad he had taken my message seriously enough to go home and get some much needed sleep!

I was convinced of our need for *more*, not less, sleep years ago when I first read Archibald Hart's book *Adrenaline and Stress*, which is now available in a second edition. In both editions he has strongly argued for the need for more sleep: an average of nine hours (eight to ten hours) a night if possible! He is absolutely convinced that most of us need at least one to two more hours of sleep than we are presently getting each night.[1]

Richard Swenson has pointed out that as a result of the discovery of electricity and the light bulb, we are now living in a twenty-four-hour-a-day society that almost never shuts down, and we are getting significantly less sleep than before. Americans are now sleeping an average of seven hours or less per night, perhaps the lowest amount of sleep than at any other time in American history. Apparently, in 1850 the average was nine and a half hours of sleep per night, but this had dropped to eight hours by 1950. Studies have found that between fifty and seventy million Americans are suffering from sleep disorders.[2]

Hart noted that a recent Gallup survey sponsored by the National Sleep Foundation showed that 49 percent of American adults have sleep-related problems, such as insomnia or difficulty falling asleep. He also pointed out that about one in six American adults suffers from chronic insomnia that lasts for more than six months and usually does not go away by itself. In another study conducted at the National Institute of Mental Health in 1993, people were given an opportunity to sleep as much as they could. The results indicated that on average those people slept eight and a half hours per night. This may have been partly due to not getting enough sleep prior to the study, and therefore needing to make up the sleep debt. Before the study, they were getting just over seven hours of sleep a night. Those who participated in the study also reported that having more sleep made them feel happier and less fatigued, with more energy. Most people, therefore, apparently need about eight and a half hours of sleep per night, a figure very close to Hart's earlier recommended nine hours![3] With sufficient sleep, we actually end up more creative, energetic, and productive.

As a result of such recent research findings, sleep is finally beginning to get some good press instead of being frowned upon. In 1999 Nancy Jeffrey wrote in the *Wall Street Journal,* "Sleep, that rare commodity in stressed-out America, is the new status symbol. Once derided as a wimpish failing—the same 1980s overachievers who cried 'Lunch is for Losers' also believed 'Sleep is for Suckers'—slumber is now being touted as the restorative companion to the creative executive mind." Jeffrey also pointed out that Netscape cofounder Marc Andreesen, Amazon.com CEO Jeff Bezos, and Snapple creator Michael Weinstein are among the leading chief executives who are regularly having at least eight hours of sleep a night.[4]

According to Swenson, a recent British study found that productivity decreases by 25 percent when people work sixty hours a week. Having adequate rest (including sleep) therefore increases productivity! It may be better to work forty-five hours a week with 100 percent productivity.[5]

### The Stress-Adrenaline-Cortisol-Serotonin-Sleep Connection

Apart from electricity and the light bulb as reasons for why we do not sleep sufficiently, according to Swenson, overstress is another cause for our not getting enough natural sleep. Hart explains that when stress goes up, adrenaline and its close cousin cortisol, the body's major stress-fighting hormones, also increase. As a result, serotonin, which is essential for good sleep, is depleted. The eventual outcome is interference with getting to sleep or getting enough sleep. With such sleep deprivation, one will not be able to cope or function as well, leading to even more stress and more cortisol and less serotonin and less sleep and more stress.... The cycle goes on and on.[6] We can break this vicious cycle through stress-management strategies, which we will cover in a later chapter. Regular physical exercise and good sleep habits are crucial components of stress management.

## Two Types of Sleep:
## REM (Dream Sleep) and Non-REM (Non-Dream Sleep)

Hart also explains that there are two main types of sleep: REM (Rapid Eye Movement) sleep, or dream sleep, that rests and rejuvenates the mind, and Non-REM sleep, or non-dream sleep, that rests and rejuvenates the body physically. Dreaming usually occurs near the end of each ninety-minute cycle of sleep. With each succeeding ninety-minute cycle, we have progressively longer periods of dreaming. We therefore need enough sleep to allow ourselves several of these ninety-minute cycles so that we can have enough REM sleep to rest and rejuvenate ourselves mentally. Nine hours of sleep each night would give us six cycles of sleep. The greatest amount of dreaming time usually occurs only after about the fifth cycle of sleep. Hart concludes that dream sleep is as crucial for our tranquility as non-dream sleep, that we may need physical exercise to feel tired enough to feel the need for more sleep, and that we need to schedule in more time for sleep.[7]

As one of the strongest advocates of sleep for our physical, emotional, mental, and spiritual well-being, acknowledging that "we need rest more today than ever before in history,"[8] Hart asserts:

> There is no greater God-given gift that can help us maintain a tranquil, non-anxious existence than sleep. Sleep is one of the most powerful healing mechanisms given to us.... Sleep simply is the best antidote for stress, and, therefore, for anxiety as well. Sleep enhances our natural tranquilizers and reverses the effects of the damage we do to ourselves through overstress.[9]

## How to Sleep Well

We may be convinced by now that we need to sleep more each night, if possible at least eight to nine hours. I, for one, will aim at increasing my average nightly sleep time to eight hours. For some of us, however, it will be a real struggle to sleep more each night, especially if we have developed poor sleeping habits, such as staying up late, sleeping inconsistently at odd hours, and sleeping only four to five hours a night. Many of us have also developed the habit of watching TV late at night, which can actually hinder our getting enough sleep. We end up getting to sleep too late, and because some TV programs may be too adrenaline stimulating, we have a harder time falling asleep. The final result is getting much less sleep than we really need.

We may have to learn some practical steps for sleeping well or for improving our sleeping habits. Hart has several helpful suggestions:

1. Go to bed and get up at the same time each day, including the weekends;
2. Try not to engage in any activity or work that results in an increase in adrenaline after a certain hour in the evening (TV watching in particular may need to be curtailed earlier);
3. Reduce the amount of light in the house as early in the evening as possible so as to have a darkened environment (which will trigger the production of melatonin, a crucial brain hormone for sleep onset);
4. Stay away from all types of stimulants (for example, caffeine, spicy foods) in the evening;
5. Do not force yourself to fall asleep;
6. Choose a quiet place to sleep;
7. Establish regular exercise in your schedule;
8. Learn and use a relaxation technique (such as slow, deep breathing, calming self-talk, and pleasant imagery, which will be described in more detail in the chapter on stress-management from a biblical perspective later in this book);
9. Unclutter or untrouble your mind before you go to bed (by writing down whatever may be bothering you so you can deal with it the next day); and
10. If you awake during the night, stay in bed unless you absolutely have to get up.[10]

Hart also points out that if we are not able to get all nine hours of sleep each night, we can always make it up by sleeping more on weekends, or taking a nap the next afternoon for the amount of sleep lost the night before. He cautions us concerning the use of sleeping pills, which may be helpful temporarily to cope with situations like bereavement or dislocation, but which may create more problems if used long-term. He also points out the risks involved in using so-called natural sleep aids, such as melatonin. They should never be used together with other prescription medications without first consulting a physician.[11] Speaking of sleep aids, but of a different kind, Swenson has emphasized the need to buy a good mattress, even if it costs more than your car![12]

It should be noted that when we first increase the amount of sleep we have each night, we may actually feel more tired the first few days upon awakening, because we are finally getting the rest we need. However, we will feel much better and more refreshed with more sleep. Of course we are referring to sleep up to about nine hours or so a night. If we find ourselves sleeping inordinate amounts of time, such as twelve to fifteen hours, and feeling fatigued or even depressed, we should consult a physician or sleep expert to see whether we may be suffering from a physical or emotional problem.

## A Biblical Perspective on Sleep

What does the Bible, God's Word, have to say about sleep? Especially since sleep takes up to a third or so of our lives! In a Ph.D. dissertation in practical theology completed at Fuller Theological Seminary in March 1999, Charles Metteer provided a comprehensive survey of what Scripture, theology, and early Egyptian monasticism have to say about a spirituality of sleep and work.[13] He noted that the Bible has much to say not only about sleep but also about a sleep-related phenomenon:

dreams. In fact, in the Old Testament, nonmetaphorical references to dreams (ninety-five texts) are actually more numerous than references to sleep (sixty-one texts).[14]

The Bible warns against the abuses of sleep, and especially sleeping too much because of laziness or to escape the responsibilities of life, including proper and productive work (see, for example, Prv 6:9-11; 20:13). However, the Bible also values *both* sleep and work or activity in proper balance (Ps 127:2; Eccl 5:12). In fact, deep and sound sleep is a blessing from the Lord, as the psalmist expressed in the following texts: "I lie down and sleep; I wake again, because the Lord sustains me" (Ps 3:5). "I will lie down and sleep in peace, for you alone, O Lord, make me dwell in safety" (Ps 4:8). "In vain you rise early and stay up late, toiling for food to eat—for he grants sleep to those he loves" (Ps 127:2).

The Old Testament has many references to dreams and their interpretation, especially to how God kept on guiding, protecting, affirming, and blessing people through dreams (see, for example, Gn 15:12-21; 20:3-7; 28:12-15; 31:3-13; 31:24; 37:5-11; 40:8-19; 41:1-7; 45:7; Jgs 7:9-28; 1 Kgs 3:5-15; 9:2; 2 Chr 1:7-13). It also emphasizes the value of dreams and the need for people to respond appropriately to dreams (see, for example, Nm 12:6; Dn 2:1-45; 4:4-27).

In Job 33:14-18, we read one of the clearest statements in the Bible on the purpose of sleep, given by Elihu:

> For God does speak—now one way, now another—though man may not perceive it. In a dream, in a vision of the night, when deep sleep falls on men as they slumber in their beds, he may speak in their ears and terrify them with warnings, to turn man from wrongdoing and keep him from

pride, to preserve his soul from the pit, his life from perishing by the sword.

God can therefore speak through dreams to steer people away from their pride and selfishness, safeguard their souls, and warn them of coming disaster. In other words, as Metteer points out, God can actively guide people during sleep through dreams, and spiritual growth can occur as a result![15]

In the New Testament, the need for sleep is assumed, although there is also some emphasis on staying awake over sleeping. For example, in the Gethsemane account, Jesus told the disciples to keep watch with Him and pray instead of sleeping (Mt 26:36-45; Mk 14:32-41; Lk 22:39-46). However, the Lord Himself was sleeping in a boat with His disciples even during a furious storm at sea, showing His unquestioning trust in His Father's care (Mt 8:23-27; Mk 4:35-41; Lk 8:22-25), as well as the appropriateness of sleeping when sleep is needed.

Metteer also noted that the New Testament has only a few direct references to dreams (Mt 1:20; Acts 2:18; Jude 8), in contrast to the Old Testament. This may be due to the coming of Jesus Christ as the full and final revelation of God, so that dreams have become less important.[16] Nevertheless, a biblical perspective on sleep and dreams still includes the appropriateness of having sufficient sleep and the importance of dreams during sleep in our relationship with God and for our spiritual growth.

Metteer makes the following insightful and helpful conclusions about sleep and dreams considered from a biblical, theological perspective:

Ultimately, falling asleep is an issue of trust.... Sleep offers us the opportunity to entrust our lives to God on a daily basis. We learn at a young age that we cannot go to sleep by our own effort.... Our inability reminds us that we cannot live by ourselves, that we were made to live in dependence upon our Maker. Sleep is thus a kind of grace—a gift from God—because we cannot will or force it upon ourselves. At those times when anxiety and stress keep us awake, we can choose to relax in the "everlasting arms" (Dt 33:27).... Sleep plays a vital role in our Christian lives.... God can profoundly influence us while we sleep.... Sleep has the mysterious ability to restore our bodies, minds, and spirits.... Spiritual restoration during sleep seems feasible due to three considerations: God does not intend for us to spend one-third of our lives in a spiritually useless activity, sleep eliminates distractions that keep us from listening to God, and dreams can challenge us to love, accept, and edify others. Indeed, it is possible that God occasionally chooses to communicate significant information to us while we sleep because we are too distracted to hear our Maker while awake.[17]

With specific reference to dreams and dreamwork to help us interpret the possible meanings of our dreams, Metteer provided several suggestions, including the following:

- preparing ourselves before we go to bed by praying for God to speak to us through a dream;
- writing down a dream as soon as possible after awakening from a dream (having pen and paper next to our bed will be helpful);
- asking ourselves key questions, such as "Why did I have

this dream?" "What issues in my life is this dream bringing up?" "What is this dream asking of me?" and reflecting on the symbolism, analogies, and images that may be present in a dream;

- realizing our fallibility in dream interpretation, and therefore doing dreamwork with families and partners, as well as within the larger Christian community, who can help us;
- asking questions about how our dreams relate to our families, churches, and communities, such as "Do my dreams confirm that I am using my gifts and talents to benefit my communities?" "Is my family, church, or community asking something of me through this dream?"
- finally, writing down what the dream experience was like and what the dream meant to us.[18]

A recent book that can further help us look at dreams and their meanings from a Christian perspective is *Windows of the Soul*, written by Paul Meier and Robert Wise.[19] Metteer also cites other helpful books in his review (see endnotes).[20] While I do believe that God can speak to us through dreams, I do not think that every dream is a special message from God or the royal road to the unconscious, as Freud proposed. We do need to take sleep much more seriously, however, and have a balanced approach to dreams and dream interpretation. In other words, sleep is crucial. And dreams may be, depending on the dream!

An interesting emphasis Metteer makes is the importance and appropriateness of napping—taking time for short periods of sleep, especially in the afternoon, or even during our times of solitude and prayer, of communion with God. He writes, "Sometimes we need a few moments of 'sacred slumber' before we can focus on our regular prayers and meditations.... Our naps dispose us to God, as do our prayers. We may also view napping as a specific act of worship."[21] In an earlier chapter, I referred to taking naps as part of resting and worship on the Sabbath. In this context we can certainly consider napping an act of worship. Sleep, including napping, is therefore "sacred slumber,"[22] a crucial means of experiencing God's rest and peace as well as spiritual formation and growth. Perhaps we could call such sacred slumber "sleeping in the Spirit"!

### Insomnia: How to Overcome It

There are times in all of our lives when we have difficulty falling asleep, or we struggle periodically with insomnia. Some of us, however, may experience chronic insomnia, over a long period of time. In that case, we should seek medical advice. Metteer points out that if the insomnia is more spiritually based, we may need to deal with causes such as stress, anxiety, fear, resentment, and bitterness. A forgiving spirit is especially important in order to have peace with ourselves, with others, and with God, particularly in dealing with any bitterness before we go to sleep (see Eph 4:26).[23]Psychologists and counselors usually suggest several guidelines for overcoming insomnia. Arnold Lazarus and Clifford Lazarus have summarized them as follows:

1. Avoid caffeine and alcohol, especially in the evening;
2. Get regular exercise such as walking without overdoing it;
3. Use your bed only for sleep and sex—avoid eating, reading, or watching TV in bed;
4. Eat some foods rich in the sleep-promoting amino acid tryptophan such as milk and poultry, if they are agreeable with you;

5. Keep the temperature in your bedroom on the cool side, because excessive heat can interfere with deep, sound sleep;

6. Keep to a consistent schedule of bed and wake times;

7. Don't force yourself to try to sleep. If you can't fall asleep fairly quickly, get out of bed and do some relaxing activity (such as reading or listening to soft music) until you feel sleepy, then go back to bed.[24]

### Resting in the Spirit

Before I end this chapter on sleep, I would like to briefly discuss a somewhat controversial phenomenon known as being "slain in the Spirit," "the falling phenomenon," or what Francis MacNutt has more aptly described as "resting in the Spirit."[25] This is a well-known phenomenon that has been reported repeatedly in revivals, as well as in revival meetings, especially in pentecostal and charismatic circles. It can also happen in a private prayer ministry session. When prayer is offered for a particular person, oftentimes with the laying on of hands on the person's forehead or shoulders, especially for the Holy Spirit's anointing and power to touch him or her, that person may fall down and experience a deep resting in the Spirit. This often occurs with tears of joy and even some shaking as the person specially experiences the love of God.

Many Christians, even from noncharismatic backgrounds, have testified how such an experience of "resting in the Spirit" has touched their hearts deeply with the love of God, and as a result has significantly transformed their lives and lifestyles. They have learned to trust God more and rest in Him more. While I am aware of the controversy surrounding this phenomenon, and I know that not all falling-down experiences are really resting in the Spirit or from God, there are occasions when people have experienced a valid, deep touch of God in this way. MacNutt's book *Overcome by the Spirit* provides a very helpful and biblically balanced approach to this phenomenon.

MacNutt states:

> I find that resting in the Spirit is a marvelous *ministry gift* that often leads people to experience the love of Jesus, lasting healing and deliverance.... I believe that God ... has a very serious purpose behind it all.... We become instantly aware that God's power is made manifest in our weakness. We are asked to let go of our controls; and we may not like that humbling fact at all. The great revivals, as we have seen, have often featured Spirit-empowered preaching accompanied by listeners falling, fainting, shouting and dropping to the ground.... Yes, being felled by the Spirit looks slightly ridiculous, as we become aware that we are weak human beings in the presence of a mighty God.... In some sense I believe God is knocking us off our feet as a kind of prophetic action to demand that we relinquish control over our lives—and over the Church—to Him.[26]

I mention this phenomenon of resting in the Spirit only to point out that God can work in many different, wonderful ways to bring us deeper into His rest and peace. Sleep is certainly one of these ways, and at times God may also cause us to rest in the Spirit to touch us deeply. Of course we should not seek an experience per se; we need always to seek God Himself. Ultimately, God works in us and among us in Christian community.

Spiritual community, or friendship and fellowship in Christ, is another crucial means of entering more fully into God's rest. The next chapter will cover this important topic.

# Nine

# Spiritual Community

Rest has many facets: physical, emotional, intellectual, spiritual, and relational. In this chapter I would like to focus on the relational (or social) aspect of rest and on spiritual community in particular as another important means of experiencing God's rest.

American Christianity, much like American society in general, tends to be highly individualistic and focused on the self. Even in matters of spirituality and spiritual formation, we often talk about how we can become more like Christ personally and individually, as if only for our own benefit and blessing! There is a danger of wanting to enter more deeply into God's rest and peace only for our own personal gain. We must understand that God has called us to a deep life in Christ not just as individuals but in the context of *Christian community:* for the sake of others and their well-being, both spiritual and wholistic! The Christian faith and the Christian walk are ultimately God-centered and other-centered, never self-centered per se, although the true self is manifested as a result. M. Robert Mulholland, Jr., defines spiritual formation as *"a process of being conformed to the image of Christ for the sake of others."*[1] He emphasizes *corporate spirituality*—our spiritual pilgrimage together as fellow members in the body of Christ—and *social spirituality*—our spiritual pilgrimage within and for the culture we live in, as God's agents of healing, transforming grace.[2] I believe it is essential for American Christians to understand this principle if we are to overcome unbiblical individualism in our spirituality.

In a helpful and important book on Christian counseling and community, Rod Wilson advocates the need to reinforce counseling through church relationships, avoiding individualistic counseling that ignores essential Christian community. Wilson states, *"Communities are central in God's economy....* We need a counseling approach that is community-oriented rather than exclusively focused on the individual. When this is the case, we will be able to appreciate the biblical emphasis on the people of God."[3]

The idea of spiritual or Christian community is so central in the Bible that Stanley Grenz, a leading contemporary theologian, has written a text on systematic theology organized around the theme or principle of the community of God. According to Grenz:

> "Community" is important as an integrative motif for theology not only because it fits with contemporary thinking, but more importantly because it is central to the message of the Bible.... Taken as a whole the Bible asserts that God's program is directed to the bringing into being of community in the highest sense—a reconciled people, living within a renewed creation, and enjoying the presence of their Redeemer.[4]

In dealing with the biblical view of human nature, Grenz

emphasizes that we are destined for community, since we are created in the image of God, who Himself dwells in a community of love as Father, Son, and Holy Spirit:

> It is not surprising that ultimately the image of God should focus on "community." As the doctrine of the Trinity asserts, throughout all eternity God is "community," namely the fellowship of Father, Son, and Holy Spirit who comprise the Triune God.... Each person can be related to the image of God only within the context of life in community with others. Only in fellowship with others can we show forth what God is like, for God is the community of love.... In the final analysis, then, the "image of God" is a community concept. It refers to humans as beings-in-fellowship.... The focal point of community can only be the community of Christ expressed in his church, which ought to be the highest form of human fellowship in this age. As we live in love—that is, as we give expression to true community—we reflect the love which characterizes the divine essence.... We live in accordance with our own essential nature, with that for which God created us. In this manner, we find our true identity.[5]

Spiritual community that includes deep, connecting, loving spiritual friendships or relationships is therefore crucial for our spiritual formation and growth individually *and* corporately! As we are involved in such spiritual community, we can experience more of God's rest and peace *from* others, as well as be channels of God's peace and rest *to* others. Wayne Muller has referred to this relational or social aspect of rest as becoming "Sabbath for one another,"[6] so that others may find rest in us, and we may find rest in others as we fellowship deeply together.

Spiritual community can include a number of things: Christian fellowship, the family, spiritual friendships, and spiritual mentoring or direction. Let's look at each of these various aspects of spiritual community, starting with fellowship.

### Christian Fellowship

Spiritual community primarily means Christian fellowship, usually in a larger church context but also in small groups, where fellow believers gather to worship God, to serve and care for each other, to pray and study Scripture together, and to reach out to the world, all with the love of Christ.

In her helpful and uplifting book originally entitled *The Hilarity of Community*, Marva Dawn emphasizes the gladness, cheerfulness, and joy that are the very essence of the hilarity that should characterize our experience of Christian community in the church. Such hilarity flows from God's amazing love for us, which transforms us into people who deeply love Him and one another as well, people with a solid hope for the future: eternity in heaven with God and His people in never-ending hilarity!!

Unfortunately, we do not often experience the hilarity of Christian community because of our tendency to be individualistic in our faith pilgrimage. As Dawn explains:

> One of the most powerful reasons for our lack of gladness is that ours is a culture of solo efforts. We live our Christian faith independently—not inextricably linked with other members of the Body of believers. Consequently, we do not experience the Hilarity of being enfolded in a moment-by-moment awareness of the good news of our hope and life in

Jesus Christ. We don't experience the support that true community engenders. We aren't free to be truly ourselves in the stewardship of our Spirit-given grace-gifts.

So I use the word *Hilarity* to describe the ideal Christian community, and my intention is to make us stop and think: what would it be like if the Christian Church were truly a community that thoroughly enjoyed being itself? It seems to me it could change the world![7]

A specific way in which we can express God's love to one another is in what Dawn calls "tenderly affectionate devotion" to each other. She especially emphasizes the need to show our loving or tender affection toward others in an appropriate, nonsexual way, and hence to have a healthy understanding of sexuality, including the valid need and expression of social intimacy.

> Much of our emptiness and perversions and violence of our culture could be dealt with more effectively if we understand our sexuality in healthy ways. The greatest need of the lonely is not for genital sex but for the security of knowing that they are cared for. They need the gentleness of an assuring touch and the warmth of someone's affirming affection. Those tired of struggling alone, of having to be solely responsible, and of carrying all their problems by themselves are helped if they can crawl into a good strong hug.[8]

We need, of course, to be culturally sensitive in this area of social intimacy and showing appropriate affection in our caring for one another in Christian community or fellowship. A hug can be very helpful and affirming if received as a caring gesture. It could be destructive and hurtful if given or received in a way that is perceived as sexually exploitive or inappropriate. Nevertheless, I agree with Dawn's emphasis on the need for all of us to be more tenderly affectionate, in an appropriate way, toward one another as loving members of the body of Christ.

In a similar vein, Henri Nouwen wrote about being daring enough to ask for help as an essential part of spiritual maturity:

> I feel within me a strong desire to live my life on my own. In fact, my society praises the self-made people who are in control of their destinies, set their own goals, fulfill their own aspirations, and build their own kingdoms. It is very hard for me to truly believe that spiritual maturity is a willingness to let others guide me.... And still, every time I am willing to break out of my false needs for self-sufficiency and dare to ask for help, a new community emerges—a fellowship of the weak—strong in the trust that together we can be a people of hope in a broken world.... To receive help, support, guidance, affections, and care may well be a greater call than that of giving all these things because in receiving I reveal the gift to the givers and a new life together can begin.[9]

True spiritual community, according to Nouwen, is therefore a fellowship of the weak. A willingness to ask for help and receive help, with vulnerability, brokenness, and humility, is essential for Christian fellowship or community.

Philip Kenneson recently wrote an insightful book on the fruit of the Spirit (Gal 5:22-23) and how to cultivate such fruit in the context of Christian community. Deep Christian fellowship produces love, joy, peace, patience, kindness, goodness, faithfulness, gentleness, and self-control. Kenneson emphasizes that God has not called us out of darkness to be conformed to the image of Christ for our own sake, but to be a light to the nations. We often speak of "possessing" the fruit of the Spirit, but Kenneson reminds us of God's larger purposes:

> If ... we cannot recognize, nourish, embody or sustain these dispositions *on our own*, then we should probably stop thinking and speaking as if these virtues are somehow our own individual *possessions*. Indeed, such ways of thinking and speaking encourage us to think of possessing these fruit or virtues as a goal to be achieved or an accomplishment to be sought, primarily for our own sakes. But this is to get things backward.... The common life of the Christian community is intended to glorify God, not the community.... Nurturing individual fruit in individual lives is not our ultimate goal. Instead, the church is called to embody before the world in all its relationships the kind of reconciled and transformed life that God desires for all of creation. This is a lofty goal and one we would be foolish to think that we could achieve apart from God's powerful working in our lives.[10]

Spiritual community in terms of Christian fellowship is therefore crucial for our spiritual growth, for cultivating the fruit of the Spirit including peace (and rest): peace with God, peace of mind and heart, and peace or harmony among fellow believers in Christ. *Attending church worship services and other meetings,* such as prayer meetings, certainly is part of Christian fellowship. However, in order to connect with each other more deeply, we will need to *meet together in small groups or cell groups, fellowships* (usually bigger than small groups but smaller than congregations), *or even house churches.* As we do so, we will be obeying the exhortation given to us in Hebrews 10:24-25: "And let us consider how we may spur one another on toward love and good deeds. Let us not give up meeting together, as some are in the habit of doing, but let us encourage one another—and all the more as you see the Day approaching."

*Christian fellowship in small groups or cell groups* has become widespread in churches all over the country and around the world. In his foreword to a helpful book on such small care groups entitled *Filling the Holes in Our Souls* (coauthored by Paul Meier, Gene Getz, Richard Meier, and Allen Doran), Don Cousins, then associate pastor at Willow Creek Community Church, wrote:

> Personally, my life has been more deeply affected in small groups than from any other source, apart from my private time with the Lord. It has been in small groups that I have developed my closest friendships and witnessed life transformation. In fact, of all the ministries that I have been involved in, none has produced greater fulfillment than that of God's activity through small groups.
>
> It would be my hope that every person would find his or her way into a small group where the real issues of life can be discussed, wrestled with, and applied in the context of both God's truth and God's people. Were that hope to become a reality, seekers would find the Savior and believers would be revitalized to live authentically in Christ.[11]

In their preface to this book, coauthors Richard Meier and Paul Meier emphasized that a healthy local church stands on three important legs:

Good Bible *doctrine,... evangelism* that brings lost people to Christ, and *fellowship* where the "one another" principles of the New Testament are practiced—loving one another, exhorting one another, confessing faults to one another, comforting one another, and rebuking one another. Every local church needs this third leg because that's where growth really takes place and where scriptural truth can really be applied.[12]

There are many different types of small groups, from a few people up to about fifteen. Sometimes a group may have a dozen or more couples, in which case it may be considered more of a fellowship group. Small groups usually meet at least once every two weeks, and many meet on a weekly basis. In some churches, small groups have replaced the traditional Sunday school classes, such as at Willow Creek Community Church in South Barrington, Illinois. Some small groups start with having a meal together, and most of them will include the following activities: worship time, Bible study, sharing and caring and prayer together. Regular attendance in a small group can help foster our spiritual growth, and the love and prayer support we experience there can keep us resting in the Lord and His grace. In a small group, we can become Sabbath or resting places for one another as we listen, carry each other's burdens, and pray together.

There are many helpful small group materials available, such as those published by Serendipity (303-798-1313, www.serendipityhouse.com); NavPress, the publishing ministry of the Navigators (719-598-1212, www.navpress.com); Zondervan (616-698-3255, www.zondervan.com); or Inter-Varsity Press (630-734-4000, www.ivpress.com). Christian Book Distributors (CBD) also has a catalog of resources and studies for small groups, at discounted prices (call **978-977-5050** for customer service).

A particularly helpful small group program for nurturing Christian growth is a RENOVARE resource entitled *A Spiritual Formation Workbook,* written by James Bryan Smith with Lynda Graybeal, with a foreword by Richard Foster, founder of RENOVARE.[13] A RENOVARE Spiritual Formation small group (usually between two and eight members) will read the following covenant aloud whenever it meets together: "In utter dependence upon Jesus Christ as my ever-living Savior, Teacher, Lord, and Friend, I will seek continual renewal through spiritual exercises, spiritual gifts, acts of service."[14] Small group members then take turns reading aloud the Common Disciplines, following the six great traditions of Christian faith (the contemplative, holiness, charismatic, social justice, evangelical, and incarnational traditions):

- By God's grace, I will set aside time regularly for prayer, meditation, and spiritual reading and will seek to practice the presence of God (the contemplative tradition);
- By God's grace, I will strive mightily against sin and will do deeds of love and mercy (the holiness tradition);
- By God's grace, I will welcome the Holy Spirit, exercising the gifts and nurturing the fruit while living in the joy and power of the Spirit (the charismatic tradition);
- By God's grace, I will endeavor to serve others everywhere I can and will work for justice in all human relationships and social structures (the social justice tradition);
- By God's grace, I will share my faith with others as God leads and will study the Scriptures regularly (the evangelical tradition);

- By God's grace, I will joyfully seek to show forth the presence of God in all that I am, in all that I do, in all that I say (the incarnational tradition).[15]

Each RENOVARE small group member then shares his or her own experience from the previous week (since the last meeting) in response to the following reflection questions, again covering the six traditions of Christian faith respectively (only the first question for each tradition will be quoted as an example):

- In what ways has God made his presence known to you since our last meeting?...
- What temptations have you faced since our last meeting?...
- Have you sensed any influence or work of the Holy Spirit since our last meeting?...
- What opportunities has God given you to serve others since our last meeting?...
- Has God provided an opportunity for you to share your faith with someone since our last meeting?...
- In what ways have you been able to manifest the presence of God through your daily work since our last meeting?...[16]

The group meeting ends with a time of sharing and praying together.

The support and accountability built into such a RENOVARE Spiritual Formation small group can be especially helpful for our spiritual growth into greater Christlikeness personally and corporately. Foster has written a comprehensive and helpful book on the six great traditions of Christian faith entitled

*Streams of Living Water*,[17] which I highly recommend for your reading.

Apart from church services and small groups or fellowships, *house churches* are another form of Christian fellowship and spiritual community. Robert Banks, in *Redeeming the Routines*, on how to bring theology to life, provides the following definition of a *house church*: "small, informal extended Christian family units which meet for church in a home." They may belong to a denomination or be independent of one. In either case, "those who gather in homes for church also gather regularly in a larger meeting, either with a cluster of independent home churches every so often or every week with other members of their congregation." Banks considers some kind of home church experience "fundamental to developing an integrated approach to life."[18]

## The Family

Spiritual community in the family context is foundational: relationships between husband and wife, parent and child, child and child, and among family members as a whole, or other extended family relationships are crucial for the development of love for God and love for one another. Spiritual growth begins at home and in the family, especially the Christian family, which is the basic unit of spiritual community. Klyne Snodgrass, in a commentary on Ephesians, wrote: "The family is the primary place for discipleship."[19] Having time together as a family for worship, prayer, Scripture reading, and sharing and caring is crucial for spiritual community and growing in discipleship or following Jesus. However, spiritual community also takes place in the humdrum, routine activities and rhythms of family life.

In a more generally spiritual but not specifically Christian vein, Victoria Moran recently wrote *Shelter for the Spirit*, focusing on how to make your home a haven in a hectic world. She provides some helpful ideas for transforming our homes into places of sacredness and comfort so that we can be refreshed and nurtured and experience more peace and rest. She introduces her book thus:

> Human beings need a place to foster an inner life. *Shelter for the Spirit* is about creating such a place from a house or apartment…. It is about reclaiming home as the primary center for our spirituality, our resourcefulness, and the majority of the best moments of our lives. It is a guide to discovering sacred space in the midst of the ordinary, and to realizing that the ordinary has been extraordinary all along…. Cleaning out a closet, eating in a little more often, snatching a few minutes alone in the morning to sit with our private plans and thoughts and feelings—such small but specific actions increase the beauty, satisfaction, and peace of mind we experience.[20]

Ernest Boyer, Jr., in *A Way in the World*, written from a more specifically Christian perspective, has provided practical suggestions for experiencing spiritual community in the family, viewing family life as a spiritual discipline that brings us closer to God and to one another in loving communion and service. We can grow spiritually together in the family and as a family, in our homes. Worship in the family is especially crucial. However, we can deepen our experience of God and His grace and peace even in the daily routines and interactions of family life.[21]

Similarly, Tim and Darcy Kimmel have described many ways to bring rest to a hurried home in their book, *Little House on the Freeway*.[22] Marshall Shelley's *The Healthy Hectic Home* is another helpful book, focusing on raising a family to love God and to love the church, in the midst of ministry that can be busy and demanding.[23]

## Spiritual Friendships and Spiritual Direction or Mentoring

Spiritual community eventually involves deep spiritual friendships between two or more fellow believers in Christ. Larry Crabb has recently emphasized the need for *connecting* spiritually and deeply with one another, whether husband to wife, brother to sister, or friend to friend. In his landmark book *Connecting*, he asserts that we have made a mistake in defining soul wounds as psychological problems requiring trained mental health specialists or therapists to treat: the real problem is not damaged psyches but disconnected souls in dire need of connection in the context of a healing community. Crabb states, "Connecting begins when we enter the battle for someone's soul. It continues as we prayerfully envision what Christ would look like in that person's life. It climaxes when the life of Christ within us is released, when something wonderful and alive and good pours out of us to touch the heart of another."[24] The inside cover of his book says:

> There is a power within the life of every Christian waiting to be released—a power that can lead to further and deeper change, a power that can help someone else join more inti-

mately to the heart of Christ, the power to heal soul wounds. That power is released by connecting with the hearts and souls of other people and allowing God's grace to flow freely through us to them.

Such deep, connecting spiritual friendships require deep love and listening to each other, and a willingness to enter into each other's struggles with brokenness and humility, as well as with prayer and spiritual direction led by the Holy Spirit. As Crabb has emphasized, the primary battle is not to solve people's problems but to really know God well and experience Christ more fully in all of our struggles and the mysteries of life.

Crabb therefore shares that when someone he loves is hurting, he prays the following prayer:

> Lord, only your life touching this person's heart can do what needs to be done. My skill, my cleverness, my knowledge add up to nothing if your life is not the energy controlling everything I do. Father, I'm overwhelmed by the awful possibilities this person is facing. I can feel the terror in my bones. But I also taste the peace beneath the terror of knowing the power of your grace. Reveal your Son through me that I might be a powerful instrument for good in your Spirit's hands.[25]

Larry Crabb and his wife, Rachael, wrote vision letters to each other. He said to her, "My vision for you is that you rest.... I want to love you so well that you rest ... more deeply rest in your Father's tender arms."[26] And Rachael wrote to Larry, "My vision for you is to see you peacefully settled—settled in who you are in Christ and in his call upon your life."[27] Rest and a peaceful settledness are longings that many couples like Larry and Rachael desire for each other. Deep spiritual friendships that connect soul to soul, or spirit to spirit, by the powerful working of the Holy Spirit, are the secret to eventually bringing such rest and peaceful settledness to our souls.

In a subsequent book entitled *The Safest Place on Earth,* Crabb expands on the need for deep, connecting spiritual friendships in the church, where more often than not such relationships do not exist because we focus on superficial programs and activities, show our goodness, and hide our failures and weaknesses due to our fear of being judged or condemned. He challenges the church as the body of Christ to be more open, vulnerable, supportive, and compassionate in dealing with the weaknesses and struggles of its members. As the inside book cover puts it:

> [The church] should be the "safest place on earth," a place of true spiritual community where people ... understand that brokenness is the pathway to a deeper relationship with God and others; connect in ways that create a passion for God deeper than all other passions; believe in the power of spiritual friendships as the best care for hurting souls; reach that sacred place of vulnerability where lives are changed forever.[28]

Crabb defines *spiritual community* as the presence of conflicted relationships met by spiritual friendship (care of the soul), and, as needed, spiritual direction (cure of the soul), characterized by dependence on the Spirit (listening to God through Word and Spirit). He further describes *unspiritual community* as the presence of conflicted relationships handled by congenial, cooperative, and consoling relationships, and as needed, by counseling or conforming relationships characterized by dependence on the flesh (figuring things out through whatever means are available).[29]

Crabb goes on to speak of the need for spiritual direction— a special kind of spiritual friendship in which a "spiritual director" gently guides a person in his or her faith journey toward a deeper life in God. He uses the term "spiritual director" because he feels that it is the best choice from the other alternatives available, such as therapist, counselor, mentor, disciple, elder, pastor, teacher, spiritual guide, or shepherd.[30]

It should be pointed out that there are times in our lives when we may still legitimately need the help of a professional counselor, therapist, or psychiatrist. Our struggles and problems in life are complex. Although we often have soul struggles that can be best addressed by spiritual friendship or more specifically spiritual direction, there are times when personal problems may require the services of trained mental health professionals. Crabb has actually suggested at least four categories of problems needing professional help:

1. Those that are caused or made worse by organic factors and/or can be significantly relieved by biological means (for example, psychotic reactions and several affective disorders like bipolar disorder and major depression);
2. Those that are due mainly to nonmoral processes of learning and conditioning (for example, educational and related behavioral problems, especially in children, and phobias/anxiety disorders);
3. Those that threaten personal or social well-being (for example, suicidal impulses and anti-social behavior); and
4. Those that are due to lack of knowledge or effective tech-

nique (for example, marital communication patterns, handling adolescent rebellion, and vocational issues).[31]

Regarding spiritual direction, Crabb writes:

> We are on a journey. Life is a journey toward a land we have not yet seen along a path we sometimes cannot find. It's a journey of the soul toward its destiny and its home. Spiritual directors are men and women who know the Spirit, who trust the Spirit, who by virtue of calling and gifting and self-awareness can see into the workings of the human soul and can direct it toward its end.... They read widely.... They love the Scriptures.... Above all, they do not manage their lives or the lives of others. They live as mystics, sensitive to the reality of Christ in them, anchored in the reality that they are in Christ. They are people who pray.... Not many of us have access to such a person. But time with a spiritual director could help scores of people.[32]

Crabb concludes: "The church is meant to be a community of spiritual friends and spiritual directors who journey together to God. We must become that community. Prayer is the starting point."[33]

There is now more material available than ever on spiritual direction or spiritual mentoring. Keith Anderson and Randy Reese recently reviewed and summarized much of this literature in a comprehensive and helpful book, *Spiritual Mentoring*, which is a guide for seeking and giving direction. They emphasize that the central action of spirituality is *"to pay attention for the presence of God in everything."*[34] Three key questions that spiritual mentors need to continually ask are, Who is God? Who am I? and What am I to do with my life? They are related to the three primary themes or empowerments a spiritual mentor will watch for in the mentoree's life: "intimacy with God, ultimate identity as a beloved child of God and a unique voice for kingdom responsibility."[35]

Anderson and Reese also cover five dynamics in the process of spiritual mentoring: attraction (initiating and establishing the mentoring relationship, including the attraction phase), relationship (developing a relationship of trust and intimacy), responsiveness (developing teachability and responsiveness in the mentoree), accountability (refining the mentoree's growth through particular accountability disciplines), and empowerment (releasing the mentoree for further growth through an empowered awareness of intimacy with God, identity as a child of God, and a unique voice for kingdom responsibility).[36] They acknowledge their debt to J. Robert Clinton, who first identified these five guiding dynamics of mentoring processes.[37]

The First International Consultation on Discipleship was held in September 1999 on England's scenic south coast. There were 450 Christian leaders representing seventy organizations from fifty countries. A *Christianity Today* editorial in the October 25, 1999, issue asserted: "Each young believer needs a mature disciple who has walked this way before and who can, in a transparent relationship, help the newer Christian toward a dual knowledge of God and self. Such relationships are not efficient, but they are essential to our growing in grace." John Stott pointed out that although we have experienced enormous statistical growth in contemporary Christianity, we do not have a corresponding growth in discipleship. Discipleship was officially defined in a statement issued by the Consultation as "a process that takes place within accountable relationships over a period of time for the purpose of bringing believers to spiritual maturity in Christ." The editorial went on to state:

> Ironically, evangelicals' penchant for methodology has both guaranteed statistical success and undermined spiritual life. "What is destroying Christianity is the marketeering of Christianity," said [James] Houston. But disciple-making is not about replicable, transferable methods, but about the mystery of two walking together. Methods treat discipleship as a problem to be solved, but mentoring treats discipleship as a relationship to be lived. Thus, Houston said, "Christian maturity is always a social, and never an individual, reality. There is no such thing as *my* maturity. There is only *our* maturity."[38]

*Spiritual community* through Christian fellowship, including church and small groups, family relationships, spiritual friendships, and spiritual direction or mentoring, in the context of deeply connecting, loving relationships with much giving and forgiving, is therefore a crucial means of spiritual growth and experiencing more deeply God's rest and grace, *for the sake of others!*

Let me end this chapter on spiritual community and rest by referring to Paul's experience of being comforted and made glad with deeper joy and peace by the visit of Titus, his close friend, spiritual partner, and fellow worker (2 Cor 8:23), as well as his protégé (Ti 1:4a). Paul says in 2 Corinthians 7:5-7:

> For when we came into Macedonia, this body of ours had no rest, but we were harassed at every turn—conflicts on the outside, fears within. But God, who comforts the downcast,

comforted us by the coming of Titus, and not only by his coming but also by the comfort you had given him. He told us about your longing for me, your deep sorrow, your ardent concern for me, so that my joy was greater than ever.

*The Message* puts it this way:

When we arrived in Macedonia province, we couldn't settle down. The fights in the church and the fears in our hearts kept us on pins and needles. We couldn't relax because we didn't know how it would turn out. Then the God who lifts up the downcast lifted our heads and our hearts with the arrival of Titus. We were glad just to see him, but the true reassurance came in what he told us about you: how much you cared, how much you grieved, how concerned you were for me. I went from worry to tranquility in no time![39]

In his writings, the apostle Paul teaches us the need to have an attitude of *servanthood*, an attitude that comes out of and contributes to the kind of deeply connecting spiritual community we have been discussing. Servanthood is another important means of resting more fully in the Lord and is the topic of the next chapter.

*Ten*

∾

# Servanthood

Our attitudes affect our feelings and behavior in significant ways. What we think influences our emotions and actions. A servant attitude is another important means of entering more fully into God's rest and peace or *shalom*. Attitudes of pride, arrogance, entitlement, and manipulative control over others rob us of God's peace and rest. An attitude of servanthood, on the other hand, enables us, by the power of the Holy Spirit, to submit to the Lord and serve Him by serving others, with humility and hiddenness, resting and rejoicing in Him who has called us to follow Him in servanthood.

Much has been written in recent years on leadership, including Christian leadership. Unfortunately, as I have read some of the literature and attended leadership conferences for pastors and church leaders, I am concerned about the models of management and leadership that we have borrowed, often uncritically, from the world. In fact, even the heavy, if not inordinate, emphasis on leadership and leadership development in contemporary Christian circles may be somewhat misplaced. While I am not against leadership and its development per se, being involved myself in training and developing church leaders, I believe that servanthood is a more foundational and central emphasis from a biblical perspective. It has often been said that the church is the hope of the world, and leaders are the hope of the church. It would be more correct biblically speaking to state that Christ through the church is the hope of the world, and *servants* are the hope of the church!

In a brief but excellent article in *World Vision Today* (Summer 1998), Steve Hayner, then president of InterVarsity Christian Fellowship U.S.A., emphasized the need for true servanthood rather than leadership per se, for playing only to an audience of One: God alone. He wrote:

> The most fundamental quality the Bible connects with godly leadership is servanthood. Learning leadership begins with learning humility, vulnerability, a willingness to do what is needed, "preferring one another," giving our lives away, and recognizing that we are stewards—never owners—of the gifts of God. Jesus repeatedly admonished his disciples whenever they talked about exerting power "The greatest among you must become like the youngest, and the leader like the one who serves" (Luke 22:26).
>
> There is a growing amount of modern literature on servant leadership. But I'm not sure I agree with leadership as the fundamental concept and servanthood as the modifier. Jesus gives an unmodified call to us to be servants—serving God and serving one another.
>
> ...Our ambition is not leadership, but servanthood. Our task is not to grow leaders, but to make disciples who will follow Jesus....
>
> How God chooses to use his servants is his concern. We

may be called to lead or to follow, to exert authority or to submit, to turn our God-given gifts in one direction or another. But that is God's business. Our identity ... and self-worth are not to be based on the roles we fill, the power we wield, or the numbers we lead. We play to an audience of one, who loves us, affirms us, and uses us.... We should long to hear from our God the words: "Well done, you good and faithful servant!"[1]

When we have the right kind of servant attitude that comes from being centered in Christ and following Him in loving humility and caring compassion for the people we serve, the Lord will keep us in His perfect peace as we steadfastly keep our mind on Him and our trust in Him alone (Is 26:3). We will not easily be offended by people who are cynical and critical of us, or upset that the people we serve are not appreciating us or noticing us. We serve the Lord as our audience of One, and therefore do not serve in order to receive the praises and affirmations of human beings who tend anyway to be fickle in both their praise as well as their criticism. We are human enough of course to enjoy and appreciate the support and encouragement of others. However, in true servanthood, we can live and serve without such affirmation, because the Lord's affirmation and loving grace are sufficient for us. We follow Him in humble servanthood, as He Himself came as the humble servant, obedient even to death on the cross for our salvation! (see Phil 2:5-11).

## Servants and Friends of the Lord

The Lord Jesus set an example for all of us to follow when He washed the feet of His disciples, as recorded for us in John 13:1-17. After He had finished washing their feet as an act of lowly, humble, loving service, He said:

Now that I, your Lord and Teacher, have washed your feet, you also should wash one another's feet. I have set you an example that you should do as I have done for you. I tell you the truth, no servant is greater than his master, nor is a messenger greater than the one who sent him. Now that you know these things, you will be blessed if you do them.

JOHN 13:14-17

The call to follow Jesus in humble and loving foot-washing servanthood to others is clear, and especially crucial for Christians to heed in today's culture. Ronald Sider, professor of theology and culture at Eastern Baptist Theological Seminary and president of Evangelicals for Social Action, wrote:

Genuine Christians embrace servanthood…. Nothing is more important today than for Christians to recover genuine servanthood…. At the center of Christianity stands a Servant…. Jesus insisted that he "did not come to be served, but to serve" (Mark 10:45)…. Jesus not only modeled servanthood, he commanded his disciples to follow in his steps. In Jesus' day, washing dusty feet was a degrading task left to slaves and social inferiors, but Jesus Himself stooped to this lowly labor … (John 13:14-15)…. It is hardly surprising that all through the rest of the New Testament, the apostles urge Christians to imitate Jesus' servanthood in every area of life.... What would happen if the church today recovered Jesus' pattern of humble service? If the church really believed Jesus' word that all who want to be disciples must imitate his servanthood?... The world would stop to watch—and be changed.... Christianity as servanthood could transform our homes and our nations. But that will never happen unless the church's leaders truly become servants.... The more faithfully Christians today follow the Servant King, the more our evangelism will have power, our marriages will have wholeness, and our societies will enjoy justice.[2]

While we have been called clearly to be servants of Jesus Christ, it is encouraging to know that He also calls us as clearly to be His friends! In John 15:15-17, Jesus says,

I no longer call you servants, because a servant does not know his master's business. Instead, I have called you friends, for everything that I learned from my Father I have made known to you. You did not choose me, but I chose you and appointed you to go and bear fruit—fruit that will last. Then the Father will give you whatever you ask in my name. This is my command: Love each other.

Jesus says we are no longer servants but friends with Him. What a friend we have in Jesus, and we are His friends too! Friendship with the Lord, or what James Houston has called "the transforming friendship"[3] founded on prayer and intimate communion with Him, is the secret to true servanthood. The Lord has called us to servanthood that comes out of deep friendship with Him, out of loving compassion. It is not servanthood out of obligation, duty, guilt, fear, or selfish motives for attention and praise.

## Servanthood Versus Servitude

True *servanthood* as discussed so far is significantly different from what Kenneth Haugk has called *servitude*. Servitude is associated with "bondage, slavery, and involuntary labor," whereas servanthood incorporates the ideas of "willingness, choice, and voluntary commitment."[4] Haugk presents four basic problems with *servitude: overidentification* (taking on the problems of the other at the expense of losing your own identity); *superficial sweetness and gushiness* (compensating for anger or frustration by covering up feelings); *being manipulated* (allowing the other to abuse your relationship); *begrudging care* (complaining about your caregiving relationships). He also describes the corresponding four appropriate and healthy responses of *servanthood: empathy* (feeling with the other while retaining good objectivity, maintaining your own identity); *genuineness* (being yourself, wounds and all; acting congruently); *meeting needs, not wants* (being straightforward about your feelings, speaking the truth in love, confronting another when necessary); and *intentionality* (choosing to be in a caregiving relationship, or getting out of it when that is the best option for all concerned).[5] In other words, servanthood is not being a doormat for everyone to walk over and abuse or manipulate, with an inability to say no to unreasonable requests, or worse still, vicious demands. Servanthood flows out of obedience to God's will, out of deep friendship and communion with the Lord, who will guide us at times to lay down our lives and sacrifice for others, and at other times to say no without feeling guilty. In true servanthood, then, we give up control to the Lord our Master and not to people.

Servanthood is not doing "random acts of kindness," as car bumper stickers have been exhorting us to do for years now. Steve Sjogren, senior pastor of Vineyard Christian Fellowship in Cincinnati, Ohio, has pointed out that such random acts should be termed "random acts of *niceness,*"[6] not kindness. Kindness is a fruit of the Holy Spirit (Gal 5:22-23), and there is nothing random or accidental about kindness! It is a fruit that the Spirit produces as we yield to Him and nurture our spiritual lives by walking with God daily and practicing the spiritual disciplines as disciplines of the Spirit. Sjogren defines this kindness as "*practical acts of mercy done by followers of Jesus who are inspired by the Holy Spirit to see others through the eyes of God.* Paul writes that 'the kindness of God leads us to repentance' (Rom 2:4). The Bible seems to distinguish between the divine quality of kindness and the human quality of niceness."[7]

Sjogren further states, "Small things done with great love can change the world."[8] In fact, he has defined "servant warfare" as "*using the power of kindness to penetrate the spiritually darkened hearts of people with the love of God.*"[9] Unfortunately, the majority of Christians do not realize that kindness can be a useful and powerful weapon of spiritual warfare! Such kindness as a key characteristic of servanthood can include doing all kinds of small things with great love for people around us, like feeding parking meters before they expire, doing free car washes, and cleaning toilets! Sjogren has called such an approach to sharing the love of Jesus in outreach to others "servant evangelism." It consists of deeds of love plus words of love plus adequate time.[10]

## True Service Versus Self-Righteous Service

True servanthood in Christ, resting and rejoicing in Him as we obey His call to serve others humbly and lovingly, results in what Richard Foster has termed "true service" as distinguished from "self-righteous service." Foster points out the following nine characteristics of self-righteous service (versus true service that flows out of true servanthood in Christ):

> Self-righteous service comes through human effort, is impressed with the "big deal," requires external rewards, is highly concerned about results, picks and chooses whom to serve, is affected by moods and whims, is temporary, is insensitive, [and] fractures community. In the final analysis ... it centers in the glorification of the individual.[11]

In contrast to these characteristics of self-righteous service, Foster provides the following description of what true service is all about:

> True service comes from a relationship with the divine Other deep inside, finds it impossible to distinguish the small from the large service, rests contented in hiddenness, is free of the need to calculate results, is indiscriminate in its ministry, ministers simply and faithfully because there is a need, is a life-style, can withhold the service as freely as perform it, [and] builds community.[12]

Foster concludes, "The risen Christ beckons us to the ministry of the towel. Such a ministry, flowing out of the inner recesses of the heart, is life and joy and peace.... Begin the day by praying, 'Lord Jesus, as it would please you bring me someone today whom I can serve.'"[13]

True servanthood involves choosing to be a servant and not just choosing to serve. The difference is crucial. Foster points out, "When we choose to serve, we are still in charge.... But when we choose to be a servant, we give up the right to be in charge. In choosing to be a servant, we submit ourselves to the Lord's bidding, to His will for us, and not our own will any longer. There is great freedom in this."[14] Foster also emphasizes that true service, especially when done in hiddenness, is most conducive to the development of humility in our character. And as pointed out earlier in this book, humility and meekness are essential for experiencing rest in the Lord (Mt 11:28-30).

## Servanthood and Retirement

In the middle of writing this book, a good friend of mine I had not seen for a few years called to say she and her husband were in town to attend a wedding and wondered if we could get together for breakfast before they left town again. I knew that saying yes would interrupt my writing schedule, but I felt it was a divine interruption and therefore a divine appointment for me to meet her for breakfast.

We had a blessed and delightful time of fellowship and prayer over breakfast when we met. She asked me to include part of what we discussed that morning in this book, as I told her about my writing on "rest." Her key questions to me were, "Is there such a thing as retirement for a Christian? Is it OK for me to slow down and rest and enjoy life more, and not think about doing things I used to do, such as writing books or speaking at seminars, or running a business?" She felt a twinge of guilt as she talked with me about retirement and slowing down her usual busy pace of life.

She was glad to hear that I believe it's definitely fine for a Christian to retire from a vocation or job, although we do not "retire" from the Christian life: we "expire" in the Christian life on earth when the Lord takes us home at death or He comes again before that happens! We had a good laugh together. We agreed that servanthood continues, even though we may be retired from our profession or vocational work. Senior citizens who are retired can still continue as servants of the Lord, doing whatever He calls them to do. They may be simpler and less hectic things that are nevertheless still very important to God and to other lives. Examples we shared included having a cup of coffee with someone who needed to talk or who might be lonely, spending more time with family members, and enjoying wasting time for God in long, leisurely communion with Him in solitude, silence, and prayer, or on longer retreats.

My friend said many of her Christian peers who are senior citizens facing retirement often struggle with some guilt for slowing down and resting more in this latter season of their lives. She does not want Christian senior citizens to feel guilty about retiring! She herself rejoiced in knowing that servanthood can continue in retirement at a slower pace of life and that this is definitely OK! In fact, it is the second half of our lives, including the latter part or season of senior citizenship, that can be the best and most blessed period of our lives because we are now older, more mature, more mellow, and wiser, or at least we hope we are! Patrick Morley has recently authored a helpful book, *Second Wind for the Second Half,* which contains twenty ideas to help you reinvent yourself for the rest of the journey in the second half of life.[15] Although written primarily for men, and for those facing midlife, Morley's suggestions can also be helpful for those of us facing retirement.

Gary Collins, in *Breathless,* describes ten traits of a life well lived:

1. *Spiritual passion:* Loving God with all your heart, soul and mind.
2. *Compassionate caregiving:* Loving your neighbors and others.
3. *Character:* Developing values and guiding principles.
4. *Balance:* Keeping equilibrium and perspective.
5. *Vision:* Living a focused, purpose-driven life.
6. *Teamwork:* Working with others to share and grow together.
7. *Adaptability:* Dealing with new trends and continual change.
8. *Soul care:* Keeping control of your lifestyle and private worlds.
9. *Growth:* Continually moving forward.
10. *Hope:* Living in the present with awareness of the future.[16]

Collins challenges us with the following conclusion that is relevant to all stages of our lives, including retirement:

Most of all, I care about living a well-lived life that pleases and brings honor to God.... I agree that the key to life is not in spending, saving, or managing time. It is more important to be investing time into causes that will have a lasting impact and into people whose lives can make a lasting difference. Ultimately, in this breathless age in which we live, the best thing you can leave behind is the example of a life well lived.[17]

## Servanthood and Suffering

Before ending this chapter, I would like to make a few comments about servanthood and suffering. True servanthood that flows from abiding in Christ means that we die daily to our self-centered ego. The way of the servant or the true disciple of Christ includes self-denial, taking up his or her cross daily, and following Jesus all the way (Lk 9:23). The way of the cross and true discipleship or servanthood is not easy: it is often difficult and painful, yet the comfort of God is available to us from the Father of compassion and the God of all comfort Himself (2 Cor 1:3-4). As we experience His deep comfort and rest, we are enabled to comfort others as well.

We can therefore embrace suffering and sacrifice as part of the servant's journey or pilgrimage of faith on earth, knowing that we will paradoxically experience God's deep comfort and gracious rest and peace in the midst of such suffering. There is the sweetness of suffering for the true servant with a servant attitude! Gary Thomas has written in *Seeking the Face of God:*

The key to understanding the sweetness of suffering is a will fully submitted to the sovereignty of God, and a clear understanding that, as Paul wrote, "our light affliction, which is but for a moment, is working for us a far more exceeding and eternal weight of glory" (2 Cor. 4:17, NKJV). The difficulty is temporary; the benefit is eternal.... Difficulty—or to use spiritual language, the cross—has always been a part of Christian spirituality and always will be.[18]

Suffering in servanthood also helps to produce humility in the servant. Humility is essential in true Christian spirituality that is God-centered (not human-centered), based on objective truth (not subjective experience), and others-focused.[19] As Thomas puts it, "There is no truly Christian spirituality without humility.... Humility contains two truths—the lowliness of men and women and the greatness of God."[20] He further writes:

> John the Baptist was the quintessential example of a humble servant of God. He was willing to serve humbly and obscurely in the desert while God readied him for his ministry. He spoke forcefully when God exalted him to become a famous and powerful prophet, but then he willingly handed his ministry over to Christ when the time was right. May God raise up many more such servants.[21]

Finally, suffering can help us as servants of Christ to worship God more deeply and fully. I have elsewhere written, based on a sermon I preached at a Fuller Seminary Chapel, "And so suffering and worship are connected. Because suffering, if we cooperate with God in the process, enables us to become purer people—and humbler people. It is the pure and humble who have truly learned to love God for who he is and to worship him most deeply."[22] Marva Dawn has called such deep worship filled with the splendor of God "a royal waste of time," leading to genuine adoration of God and faithful spiritual formation of His people.[23] As we love and worship Him, we will experience the rest and the *shalom* of God!

Although we often speak about the cost of discipleship or truly following Jesus all the way as His servant, we must remember that the cost of nondiscipleship is immensely greater! It is deep wisdom to walk with Jesus daily and follow Him in true discipleship and servanthood. Dallas Willard, in *The Spirit of the Disciplines,* wrote:

> But the cost of nondiscipleship is far greater—even when this life alone is considered—than the price paid to walk with Jesus.
>
> Nondiscipleship costs abiding peace, a life penetrated throughout by love, faith that sees everything in the light of God's overriding governance for good, hopefulness that stands firm in the most discouraging of circumstances, power to do what is right and withstand the forces of evil. In short, it costs exactly that abundance of life Jesus said he came to bring (John 10:10). The cross-shaped yoke of Christ is after all an instrument of liberation and power to those who live in it with him and learn the meekness and lowliness of heart that brings rest to the soul…. The correct perspective is to see following Christ not only as the necessity it is, but as the fulfillment of the highest human possibilities and as life on the highest plane.[24]

Servanthood, reflecting true discipleship, with a genuine Spirit-inspired servant attitude, expressed in true service and not self-righteous service, is therefore another significant means of entering more fully into God's rest.

# Eleven

# Stress Management:
# A Biblical Perspective

S tress management has become a household word in American society. It is seen as an essential part of life, precisely because life is now too stressful: accelerated beyond even hurried and often overloaded to the point of sheer exhaustion and fatigue, nearing collapse! For many Americans, any semblance of rest and serenity in an age of anxiety and stress requires mastery of stress-management strategies and techniques. While stress-management methods can be helpful, they need to be placed in proper perspective from a biblical viewpoint. This chapter will provide both practical steps for stress management as well as a biblical critique and perspective. Entering into God's rest and *shalom* includes learning to manage stress or overstress, but it goes beyond stress management to Spirit-filled living, which makes the best of stress so that life's hassles can be used by God to form and cultivate the fruit of the Spirit, as Mark McMinn has wisely pointed out.[1]

Donald Meichenbaum, a well-known clinical psychologist and key figure in the field of cognitive-behavioral therapy, who developed Stress Inoculation Training some years ago, wrote:

One of the major growth industries in North America is that of books and workshops on stress reduction and prevention. These nostrums take one of two formats—they either advocate one specific stress management technique such as meditation, relaxation, and aerobic exercise, or they espouse an eclectic approach consisting of an array of techniques that usually includes relaxation (the "aspirin" of the stress reduction field), meditation and biofeedback training, drugs, cognitive approaches, time management procedures, dietary and life-style changes and training in interpersonal assertiveness and values clarification. These procedures are usually offered in an atheoretical framework, and they convey the flavor that there is a "right" way to cope or adjust.[2]

There is, of course, no one right way to cope or adjust to stress because there are significant individual differences among people and their perceptions of stress, as well as their coping capacities and styles of responding to stress. Let's first define stress more clearly before we go on to practical methods for stress management or stress reduction.

## What Is Stress?

Stress is an overused term that is not easy to define. The late Hans Selye, father of stress research, described stress as the non-specific *response* of the body to any demand made on it, or more simply as "the rate of wear and tear in the body."[3] He also coined the terms "eustress" or good stress (for example, experiencing joy or fulfillment) and "distress" or bad stress (with excessive levels of damaging stress).[4] Stress, in Selye's view, is therefore part and parcel of life itself: stress is inevitable and unavoidable as long as one is alive!

Whereas Selye put the emphasis on the *response* of the body in defining stress, others have focused more on the *stimuli* or *environmental events* that may be noxious or stressful to us. Thomas Holmes and Richard Rahe focused on major life events, whether positive or negative (for example, death of a spouse, divorce, marriage, retirement, vacation, Christmas) in defining stress, when they first described their Social Readjustment Rating Scale in 1967.[5] Jeffrey Bjorck has pointed out that subsequent research has shown that only the stressful life events perceived as negative are crucial for predicting maladjustment.[6] Furthermore, psychologist Richard Lazarus has found that it is daily hassles rather than major life events that add the greatest pressure to life. The top ten hassles in life according to Lazarus and summarized by McMinn are (from one to ten): concern about weight; health of family members; rising prices of common goods; home maintenance; too many things to do; misplacing or losing things; yard work or outside home maintenance; property, investment and taxes; crime; and finally, physical appearance.[7]

A third and more prevalent view of stress is the *transactional* perspective, which Meichenbaum describes as follows:

> Stress is viewed as neither a stimulus nor a response, but rather as the result of a *transaction*, influenced by both the individual and the environment. From a transactional perspective, stress is defined as a cognitively mediated relational concept. It reflects the relationship between the person and the environment that is appraised by the person as taxing or exceeding his or her resources and as endangering his or her well-being.[8]

Such a view is based on the seminal work of Richard Lazarus and his colleagues, including Susan Folkman.[9] Bjorck summarized their transactional perspective on stress thus:

> They define stress as occurring when one comes to view one's transactions with the environment as involving threat, harm, or loss, or challenge that strains personal resources. This perceptive process is labeled appraisal, and stress vulnerability is dependent on it.... Appraisal involves three phases.... In primary appraisal, the individual evaluates the extent to which an event is irrelevant, harmless, positive, or stressful. Stressful events are further appraised as potentially harmful (threatening), actually harmful (that is, involving harm or loss), or potentially beneficial (challenging). When events are viewed as stressful, secondary appraisal follows, whereby adequacy of personal coping resources is assessed.... Distress is directly dependent on these appraisals.[10]

For the sake of clarifying the meaning of stress, Archibald Hart, who has written a number of significant books on stress management from a Christian perspective, has offered the following suggestion:

> One way to solve this labeling problem is to refer to all stimulation that is healthy and normal as "simple arousal." Stimulation that is above normal but not necessarily harmful we can call "stress" or "overarousal." And stimulation that is both excessive and damaging we can call "distress" or "excessive arousal."... *The only good stress is stress that is short-lived.* Even simple arousal, if prolonged, will cause stress problems. And extreme states of distress, if prolonged, nearly always

produce serious stress damage, especially to the cardiovascular system.[11]

More recently, Hart has termed excessive arousal "overstress." He noted that overstress costs our society at least sixty billion dollars a year as a result of its consequences, such as lost productivity, medical care required for stress-related disorders, job accidents, and traffic fatalities.[12]

Hart emphasizes that *overstress* occurs due to *adrenaline flooding*, in which the adrenal glands produce too much of the emergency stress hormones to help mobilize your body for a fight-or-flight response when you are experiencing stress, especially for a prolonged period of time. Serious effects follow this adrenaline flooding, such as an increase in blood cholesterol, narrowing of blood vessels, and an increase in blood-clotting tendencies. Short bursts of adrenaline arousal make life exciting and are not damaging in the short term, but prolonged periods of such arousal *are* damaging, and this is what overstress is all about. Hart asserts that the answer to combating overstress is to pace ourselves in a balanced way so that we learn to live on less adrenaline overall, including giving ourselves time to slow down and recover after short periods of intense stress.[13] He points out that not only distress but too much eustress over a long enough period of time will have deleterious effects on our health.[14] Even pleasant experiences can be stressful, and hence too much of a good thing for a long time can be bad, resulting in overstress or adrenaline flooding. Hart has noted the following symptoms of overstress, based on a research study by Jonathan C. Smith and Jeffrey M. Seidel of Roosevelt University: gastric distress (for example, stomach discomfort, pain, excess secretion of acid, and churning); disturbed cardiorespiratory activity; restless activity;

self-conscious activity; feelings of fatigue and lack of energy; headaches; backache; skin difficulties; shoulder, neck, and back tensions; and trembling and shaking.[15]

Psychologists Robert Woolfolk and Frank Richardson have provided another definition of stress that is quite widely accepted: "Stress is a perception of threat or expectation of future discomfort that arouses, alerts, or otherwise activates the organism."[16] In this definition, there are three main components of the stress reaction: the environment or environmental events, the appraisal and evaluation of the environment, and the reaction of physiological/emotional arousal. In order to manage or control stress effectively, all three components of stress need to be addressed. The emphasis in this definition of stress is on the appraisal and evaluation component: stress is ultimately a *perception* of threat or an *expectation* of future discomfort that has some physiological or emotional effects. Our thinking is therefore crucial in how we experience stress and how we cope with it. This view is consistent with the transactional perspective on stress that includes a strong cognitive-evaluative, or thinking, component. Hart emphasizes, however, that even if one does *not* perceive threat or expect future discomfort but experiences eustress, too much of such good stress for too long still leads to overstress, or adrenaline flooding, with eventual stress damage.

## How to Manage Stress

Stress-management strategies and techniques abound, and there are many books available to help you control or reduce stress and thus prevent overstress.[17] Let's briefly review the major methods for stress management, to help you learn to handle stress more effectively and to grow through stress so that you can experience God's peace and rest more fully. Life is inevitably stressful, but it does not have to be so often in over-stress mode. It should be noted that secular books on stress management or stress reduction often include a number of stress-control techniques that many Christians will not feel comfortable using, such as transcendental meditation (TM) and self-hypnosis.

The following stress-management techniques, taken together, deal with all three components of stress: the environment or environmental events, appraisal and evaluation of such events, and physiological/emotional arousal (especially adrenaline arousal).

Some years ago Gary Collins wrote *You Can Profit from Stress*, in which he offered several suggestions for stress reduction: (1) don't play roles—be yourself; (2) choose your friends wisely; (3) don't let things drift or be postponed—deal with them; (4) admit your fears and face them; (5) make time to get away and relax; (6) do something for others; (7) be willing to compromise and negotiate; (8) work on a *realistic* self-image; (9) do what is right—don't cheat, lie, or be immoral—admit your faults, and confess your sins; (10) take one thing at a time—set priorities and steps of action; then cross them out when they are finished; (11) seek a *balance* in your life (for example, work, leisure, exercise, contemplation, resting and sleep, and proper nutrition); (12) be *realistic*—some things you *cannot* change; (13) recognize the tension-reducing value in swimming (or jogging), relaxing music, casual reading, watching TV, and other diversionary activities, when practiced in moderation; (14) slow down—move, eat, and talk more slowly, to feel less pressured; (15) avoid excuses—take responsibility for yourself and your own actions; and (16) talk things over—with a friend, relative, pastor, or counselor.[18] It may be interesting to note that, in some preliminary research with women subjects, social support like this has recently been found to increase the body's levels of oxytocin, an antistress hormone, in stressful situations.

More recently, Hart has offered the following helpful guidelines for managing stress effectively or preventing stress buildup in your life: (1) set boundaries in your life; (2) resolve conflicts quickly; (3) complete unpleasant tasks first; (4) "inoculate" yourself against stress by dealing with small amounts of stress in an effective way; (5) firmly set up "recovery times" after particular periods of stress; (6) minimize your level of adrenaline arousal; (7) have open and healthy relationships; (8) learn to say no and give yourself a break; (9) postpone making major decisions in times of stress; and (10) use spiritual resources for stress busting.[19]

Hart also makes several suggestions for recovering from a chronic state of adrenal exhaustion due to overstress: (1) minimize stress as much as possible by simplifying your lifestyle, taking up a hobby, and getting plenty of sunshine and fresh air; (2) have at least eight and a half to nine hours of sleep each night (remember that Hart believes sleep is the best antidote for stress and anxiety); (3) stay away completely from caffeine, nicotine, alcohol, and recreational drugs; (4) do not eat foods that may cause allergies or upset your digestive system; (5) take vitamins like B-complex, C, and E to supplement your diet; and (6) treat life with more respect and take yourself less seriously.[20]

In the crucial area of our thinking, we need to renew our minds according to God's truth in Scripture (Rom 12:2) so that we appraise or evaluate circumstances and environmental events more biblically and realistically without unnecessary or undue stress (Phil 4:8). In other words, it is not only what happens to us but what and how we think about it that determines our emotional and physiological reaction, and our behavioral response. *Cognitive restructuring* is the technical term for changing negative, extreme, unrealistic, irrational, distorted thinking, especially *catastrophic* thinking ("This is too much! I can't take it anymore. It's the end of the world!") into more realistic, accurate, positive, and biblical thinking ("Just relax. Take it easy. With God's help I can handle it. It's not the end of the world. No point worrying. God is in control. Let me pray and trust Him fully."). William Backus and Marie Chapian have called this "telling yourself the truth" based on Scripture (Jn 8:32).[21]

Hart, in another book, *Habits of the Mind,* describes ten habits of a healthy mind:

1. See the good in others;
2. give yourself permission to fail;
3. keep your conscience clear;
4. don't punish yourself;
5. value life's little blessings;
6. accentuate the positive;
7. be the right sort of optimist;
8. accept yourself for who you are;
9. stay in touch with reality; and
10. cherish God's love and wisdom.[22]

John Ortberg and I wrote a couple of books on depression a few years ago, in which we suggested several helpful ways of coping effectively with depression.[23] Many of the methods we described are also helpful for managing stress and anxiety. Here are some examples:

- *inner healing prayer;*
- *learning to be assertive* (for example, learning to say no to unreasonable demands without feeling guilty);
- *relaxation and coping skills* such as those used in stress-inoculation training, like *slow, deep breathing* (take in a slow deep breath, hold it for a few moments, then breathe out slowly), *calming self-talk* (for example, "Just relax. Take it easy. Allow the tension to unwind. With God's help I can handle this."), and *pleasant imagery* (for example, lying on the beach or taking a walk in the woods);
- *listening to music* that is soothing and inspirational;
- *taking care of the body* by practicing good *nutrition* (for example, a well-balanced diet with sufficient vitamins and minerals), regular *exercise* (for example, fast walking or swimming for half an hour three times a week); and having adequate *sleep* (for example, eight to nine hours each night);
- *cognitive restructuring;*
- *prayer with thanksgiving* (Phil 4:6-7);
- *humor* (Prv 15:15; 17:22);
- *self-help reading;*
- *contemplative prayer and meditation on Scripture.*[24] Meditation on Scripture, with a deep love for God's Word, leads to great peace and well-being: "Great peace have they who love your law" (Ps 119:165a).

I have described several methods for managing chronic pain that are also useful for stress management and tension reduction, such as relaxation techniques, cognitive coping skills, cognitive therapy methods or cognitive restructuring based on Scripture, stress-inoculation training, pacing and pleasurable activities, psychotherapy, support groups, prayer, solitude and private retreats, other spiritual disciplines, meditation on Scripture (using David Ray's steps for Christian meditation), and fellowship and worship.[25]

Edward Charlesworth and Ronald Nathan, in their comprehensive book *Stress Management,* written from a more general, secular perspective, covered virtually all the main methods for stress management, including:

- *relaxation techniques,* such as progressive relaxation, autogenic phrases and images, and imagery training;
- *life-change management:* changing Type A behavior (for example, time urgency, impatience, hostility) to more Type B behavior by setting priorities, slowing down, and calming down anger or hostility;
- *cognitive restructuring:* taking the stress out of what you tell yourself with calming, coping self-talk;
- *dealing effectively with anxiety and anger;*
- *learning to be appropriately assertive in communicating your needs and feelings;*
- *time management;*
- *keeping your body "tuned up" and safe* (with regular exercise and keeping fit);
- *nutrition and weight control;*
- *support groups* to help you through crises;
- *religion* as a source of strength;
- *professional counseling or psychotherapy* when and if needed.[26]

It is interesting to note that Charlesworth and Nathan included religion as a source of strength that can help one manage stress more effectively. In fact, research has shown that overall there is a positive relationship between religion or spirituality and both physical and mental health.[27] Donald Meichenbaum and Deborah Fitzpatrick noted the various forms religious coping can take: turning to God or trusting God, using prayer, confession, seeking support from clergy or a congregation, and focusing on the world to come or life hereafter. Citing the work of psychologist Kenneth Pargament, they pointed out that religious belief, faith, and rituals have been found to (1) make stressful events more bearable by providing a meaningful and coherent worldview; (2) offer a source of hope and comfort, as well as clear direction for coping with stressful situations; and (3) nurture a sense of belonging and a sense of support and intimacy with God and with other members of the religious community.[28]

Even secular researchers and psychologists like Meichenbaum are therefore acknowledging the positive effects religious belief or faith can have on coping and managing stress effectively.

I have reviewed a long list of stress-management methods that can be helpful for reducing stress and adrenaline arousal, and therefore for experiencing more of God's rest and *shalom*. The spiritual means of entering more fully into His rest that I covered earlier in this book are crucial for stress management from a biblical perspective: Shepherd-centeredness, Spirit-filled surrender, solitude and silence (including contemplative prayer), simplicity, Sabbath, sleep, spiritual community, and servanthood. However, as Mark McMinn has rightly pointed out, we need to go beyond stress management as commonly understood and practiced (which sometimes gets reduced to stress elimination). We need to learn to make the best of stress from a biblical perspective and allow life's hassles and trials to cultivate or form in us virtuous character, which is the fruit of the Spirit: love, joy, peace, patience, kindness, generosity (goodness), faithfulness, gentleness, and self-control (Gal 5:22-23).

## Beyond Stress Management:
## Making the Best of Stress

Stress is an inevitable part of life. As long as we have breath and are alive, we will experience some stress. Stress management helps us to control or reduce our stress so that it does not go into overstress at all, or for too long a period of time. Stress cannot be eliminated totally as long as we are alive. In fact, some stress is good for us, in motivating us to live more productively. The danger in overemphasizing stress management is that we get too caught up in trying to reduce our stress levels and adrenaline arousal, sometimes to the point where we even try to eliminate *all* stress, which is not possible this side of the kingdom! We do need to be responsible and take appropriate steps of faith and action, though, with God's help, to manage stress more effectively in our lives, especially if we are often driven to overstress. It is biblical to aim at making the best of stress so that God can nurture and form the fruit of the Spirit in us, which is ultimately Christlikeness (Rom 8:29). Jesus promised that in this world we will face trouble: He also told us to take heart and be encouraged because He has overcome the world and we can have peace in Him! (Jn 16:33).

McMinn has some wise words for us in this regard:

If virtuous character helps us to respond constructively to stress, how do we develop virtuous character? Through stress…. It is better to think of character and stress as inseparable…. Everyone wants virtue, but no one wants stress…. Stress and virtue go hand in hand. We can't know virtue without knowing stress, and we cannot respond well to stress without having virtue.[29]

McMinn also notes that hardy personalities are less likely to be ill during times of stress. He cites the work of stress researcher Suzanne Kobasa on the stress-resistant hardy personality (with an internal locus of control, commitment to life activities, and viewing change as challenge) and subsequent research by others. He concludes that such findings help to explain why stress and illness are only weakly related (it is a myth that stress is *always* bad or that stress *always* causes illness). The research suggests that our *character* or personality is causal in determining how stress affects us.[30]

McMinn further states:

Another approach is to see stress not as our enemy, but as a reminder of our enemy. Stress points to our weaknesses…. Stress doesn't always reflect personal sin, but all stress reflects human fallenness…. Our goal is not to eliminate stress but to manage it by establishing self-awareness and virtue in the context of healthy relationships. Stress will always be with us, reminding us of our need, pushing us beyond our shallow self-sufficiency, pointing us to the One greater than ourselves…. Stress points us toward redemption…. Thriving in the midst of stress requires us to trade in our worship of happiness and our postmodern beliefs about stress for an older model: *I want to be blessed with virtuous character, and God shapes my character through trials and the community of truth....* Throughout Scripture we see virtue valued above happiness and stress reduction.... Stress isn't a bad thing that should always be avoided; it can be God's tool to shape our character.... Stress helps us to understand our need for God. It allows us to understand our weakness so that we can know God's strength.[31]

McMinn therefore emphasizes that stress humbles us, but through it God gives us grace to make us whole and to grow virtuous character in us.

Ray Anderson also recently wrote on acquiring the virtues we most admire in *Living the Spiritually Balanced Life*, encouraging us to keep virtue from turning bad due to a lack of balance or overemphasis. He describes fourteen Christian virtues in this way:

1. *self-control:* being angry without losing your temper;
2. *self-confidence:* being assertive without being aggressive;
3. *courage:* overcoming fear without being foolhardy;
4. *compassion:* showing mercy without condoning wrong;
5. *generosity:* giving freely without giving yourself away;
6. *kindness:* taking care without taking control;
7. *wisdom:* loving freely without loving foolishly;
8. *honesty:* being truthful without shaming others;
9. *tolerance:* being agreeable without agreeing with every-thing;
10. *flexibility:* being strong without being rigid;
11. *serenity:* being calm without being detached;
12. *faith:* being visionary without going out of focus;

13. *hope:* being optimistic without being unrealistic; and

14. *love:* going the second mile without going out of bounds.[32]

In a similar vein, Gary Thomas has written *The Glorious Pursuit* about embracing the virtues of Christ or the classical virtues: humility, surrender, detachment, love, chastity, generosity, vigilance, patience, discernment, thankfulness, gentleness, fortitude, obedience, and penitence.[33]

In *Finding Contentment*, Neil Clark Warren emphasizes that authenticity is the foundation of all true contentment that goes beyond momentary happiness. Such contentment is an essential part of experiencing God's rest. Warren believes that there are ten major characteristics of authentic people who know deep contentment: (1) they live in the present; (2) they are free of fear; (3) they are not judgmental; (4) they genuinely appreciate themselves; (5) they hunger for the truth; (6) they are adaptable and flexible; (7) they have a strong sense of gratitude [which is at the very heart of contentment according to Lewis Smedes]; (8) they love to laugh and are lighthearted; (9) they exhibit a high degree of dignity; and (10) they sleep well![34]

## Some Biblical Principles for
## Stress Management and Beyond

Let me now share with you several passages from Scripture that provide us with some biblical principles that will help renew our thinking and thereby enable us not only to manage stress but grow through stress.

*1. Romans 12:2; Philippians 4:8; Psalm 43:5.* We need to be transformed by the renewing of our *minds* or thinking: to tell ourselves the truth from Scripture and focus on what is true, noble, right, pure, lovely, admirable; to choose to think on these things that are excellent or praiseworthy. This is the biblical basis for Christian cognitive restructuring!

*2. Matthew 6:25-34; 1 Peter 5:7; Psalm 55:22; Romans 8:35-39; 1 John 4; Isaiah 41:10; 43:1-4; Zephaniah 3:17; Deuteronomy 33:27; Psalm 23.* These passages from Scripture emphasize God's love and care for us and our preciousness and worth to God. Yet, in this fallen world, trials and difficulties, including stress, are part of life, but we can grow through them as the Lord helps us (Jn 16:33; Jas 1:2-4; Phil 4:13). Even the stress or struggle of spiritual warfare against the devil (1 Pt 5:8-9) and spiritual forces of evil (Eph 6:11-12) can be an experience of victory and growth through submitting to God and resisting the devil (Jas 4:7), learning to be strong in the Lord and His mighty power, and using the armor of God, especially prayer and the Word of God (Eph 6:10-18). We can rest in the Lord, even in spiritual warfare, knowing that He has already won the spiritual victory for us (Col 2:15; Heb 2:14). The Lord has often reminded me, from Old Testament texts, that the battle is His, not mine: He will undertake for us and bring victory and deliverance (2 Chr 20:15, 17; 1 Sm 17:47). Not by might nor by power, but by His Spirit! (Zec 4:6). As the Lord told Moses, so He reassures us afresh: "My Presence will go with you, and I will give you rest" (Ex 33:14).

*3. Matthew 11:28-30; Luke 10:38-42.* Jesus will give us rest, but we need to have humility and meekness and come to Him and sit at His feet, spending or "wasting" time with Him, listening to His voice.

*4. Mark 6:31.* We need to take time off to rest, as well as to keep the Sabbath weekly for ceasing from work, resting, and worshiping (Ex 20:8-11; Dt 5:15; Mk 2:27).

*5. 1 Corinthians 13.* Love is the key to what really counts in life from God's eternal perspective and not from materialistic criteria of success. *A correct biblical perspective on true success is crucial for managing stress and growing through it.* Following materialistic, external criteria of success that reflect underlying human pride or egomania is a sure way to experience overstress and eventual downfall. Vernon Grounds, over two decades ago, wrote a powerful article on the need for faith to face worldly failure and see that worldly success is not such a great thing after all! He wrote, "In each of us there is a desire for recognition, a desire to be important or influential … to be noticeably superior."[35] The apostle John calls this the "pride of life" (1 Jn 2:16, KJV). Grounds went on to say that evangelical Christians are bowing before the "bitch goddess" of worldly success, and being sinfully preoccupied with statistics and numbers—with the size of our sanctuaries, salaries, and Sunday schools, and with statistics about our budgets, buildings, buses, and baptisms. Worldly success has crept right into the church and Christian ministries!

Grounds challenges us with the following conclusion that needs to be repeated afresh to a new generation of Christians who may be even more seduced today by worldly success:

> Most of us will work without ever becoming well known. Do we have faith to face failure? Do we really believe that worldly success is wood, hay, and stubble? We need to remember how often the Church will judge us the way the

world does. Before anyone decides on a full-time ministry, for example, they must realize that God may be calling him or her to a ministry of tedious mediocrity. Regardless, God's approval is the most important part. It is far more important to follow God's blueprint for your life than to be another Billy Graham, or Hal Lindsey, or Robert Schuller, or Bill Bright. Each of us needs the faith to cling to biblical principles of success despite possible worldly failure. And each of us must have the faith to keep serving even if unappreciated, unsung, and unapplauded—in short, we need the faith to face failure.[36]

A biblical perspective on success will emphasize the following criteria: *Christlike agape love* (1 Cor 13:1-8; Jn 13:34-35) and not pulpit eloquence, communication skills, penetrating insight, remarkable gifts, encyclopedic knowledge, or even mountain-moving faith, as Grounds pointed out; *servanthood and humility* (Mt 20:25-27); *faithfulness* (Mt 25:21); *obedience to God and His Word* (1 Sm 15:22; Jos 1:7-9; Mt 7:24-29); *vulnerability and strength in weakness* (2 Cor 12:9-10); *doing our best as unto the Lord* (Col 3:23); and *becoming more like Jesus* (Rom 8:29). It is essential for us to understand that God's ways and standards are often different from our human ways and standards: His ways and thoughts are higher and better (Is 55:8-9). God judges the *heart:* internal motives are critical, and whatever is highly valued by the world is detestable in God's sight (Lk 16:15)!

*6. Habakkuk 3:17-19.* The true basis of life and fulfillment is *the Lord Himself and Him only!* Let us learn to *rejoice in the Lord and be joyful in God our Savior,* despite difficult or bad circumstances, and have our deepest satisfaction in Him. Praise and worship of God are powerful stress busters!

7. *Philippians 4:4-9.* To overcome anxiety and overstress, *rejoice in the Lord always* (v. 4); *be gentle* (v. 5); *pray with thanksgiving* (vv. 6-7); *think biblically* (v. 8); and *act appropriately* (v. 9).

8. *Romans 8:28.* Know and believe God's blessed assurance that in all things, He works for the good of those who love Him, who have been called according to His purpose. There is ultimate meaning and good in our lives. Our present suffering cannot be compared to the glory that shall be revealed in us and in heaven to come (Rom 8:18; 2 Cor 4:16-18).

## Stress and Burnout

It should be noted that *stress* is *not* the same as *burnout.* We have heard much about burnout since the term was first introduced to the scientific literature in the early 1970s by Herbert J. Freudenberger, as well as by Christina Maslach. Ayala Pines, another renowned researcher on burnout, noted that definitions of burnout vary somewhat, but here are two examples: "burnout is a syndrome of emotional exhaustion, depersonalization, and reduced personal accomplishment that can occur among individuals who do people work of some kind," according to Christina Maslach. Ayala Pines and Elliot Aronson have defined burnout as "a state of physical, emotional, and mental exhaustion caused by long term involvement in emotionally demanding situations."[37] Burnout is therefore a syndrome of reactions to being chronically involved in emotionally demanding situations with people.

Pines pointed out that burnout is different from stress:

> Stress happens to more people and in more situations than burnout. Everyone can experience stress but burnout can only be experienced by people who entered their careers with high ideals, motivation, and commitment.... Unlike stress, which can occur in almost any type of work, burnout occurs most often among those who work with people.... Nevertheless, stress as such does not cause burnout. People are able to flourish in stressful and demanding jobs if they feel their work is significant and appreciated.[38]

While stress and burnout are not identical, suggestions for managing stress are often the same ones made for preventing and managing burnout.[39]

## Two Closing Stories

To conclude this chapter, I would like to share with you two true stories. The first has to do with what I experienced as I was writing this chapter and the previous two over a period of three weeks or so. During this time, I was hoping for some quiet, uneventful time so that I could focus on completing these three chapters on spiritual community, servanthood, and stress management. It did not turn out that way. Instead, these past three weeks have been busy and stressful with a number of difficult events that occurred: a church member died suddenly of a heart attack, followed by the memorial service as well as ministry to the bereaved spouse and family members; a church staff member broke her ankle when she tripped and fell; a church member had her baby early, and another had a miscarriage; discovering another diagnosis of cancer in a relative of a close friend; finding out that the church property my church was bidding for in a church-planting plan had other higher bids for it; hospitalization of a close friend; death of another church member's relative; and in the last couple of days, even as I am writing this, there has been a huge fire burning in the mountains just north of where I live in Arcadia, California! Thank God the fires have been contained by the excellent work of firefighters and helicopters dropping great amounts of water. A week ago there was a similar dangerous fire in the city of Glendale, where our church is located. One of our pastoral staff members and his family had to be evacuated. We all prayed much, and the fire was finally put out without any damage to people or property. There has also been much prayer for protection regarding the Arcadia area fires, which now have been controlled, praise God! I was also called up for jury duty a day ago but fortunately was not selected, so I can continue my plan to finish writing this book by the end of December 1999!

I should be really stressed out or into overstress as a result of having to face such a list of demanding environmental events in about three short weeks—plus the pressure of finishing my writing to meet the deadline for this book! It has been difficult and tiring, but I do not feel overwhelmed or overstressed. By the grace of God, I have been enabled by the Holy Spirit to remain centered in the Lord. He has assured me through His Word that He is in control of things and that He will give me sufficient strength and grace to do His will, including completing the writing of this book.

I have continued to tell myself such truth and trust God's promises from His Word. I have prayed and waited upon Him in solitude and silence and read His Word. I have also been in regular spiritual community and fellowship with my family and church friends, pastoral staff, and intercessors. I have really appreciated the love and powerful prayer support of these special friends who pray for me daily. I have experienced God's rest and peace in the midst of such stressful situations! As a result, I have been able to continue my writing according to schedule, despite the many divine interruptions, which I have viewed as divine appointments to serve Him and other people.

Resting in the Lord is a reality that can be experienced in the midst of stress. And, of course, the adrenaline arousal can be slowed down because of the rest experienced in Him. I will need to schedule in some more rest and downtime, including having even more sleep, after I finish writing the next chapter of the book, which is the last one.

According to Archibald Hart, my colleague and good friend at Fuller Seminary, this is wisdom in stress management: to plan adequate recovery time, including sufficient sleep, after a period of stress. I should point out that not going to the malls for Christmas shopping, some fasting from watching TV, and not writing Christmas cards till much later helped a lot! My wife and two teenage children have also been very patient and understanding in shielding me from other demands on my time during this period of writing. They have gone out and done the Christmas shopping! There were, however, a number of Christmas programs and meetings that I still attended as the pastor of the church. As McMinn has advocated, I have made the best of stress during these weeks, and grown through stress to rest in the Lord more fully and trust Him more deeply.

The next story is another true story, originally told by Philip Yancey in his excellent book *The Jesus I Never Knew*. His wife

Janet worked with senior citizens, half of them white and the other half black, in their seventies and eighties in age, near a Chicago housing project that is apparently the poorest community in the United States. Janet noticed a significant difference in the way the two groups of senior citizens faced death, with some exceptions. The whites increased in their fear and anxiety, and complained about their lives, families, and worsening health. The blacks, however, were able to keep up a triumphant spirit and good humor, although they had every reason to be in despair and bitterness. In Yancey's own words:

> What caused the difference in outlooks? Janet concluded the answer was hope, a hope that traced directly to the blacks' bedrock belief in heaven.... I am convinced that for these neglected saints, who learned to anticipate and enjoy God in spite of the difficulties of their lives on earth, heaven will seem more like a long-awaited homecoming than a visit to a new place.... Jesus offers a promise of a time, far longer and more substantial than this time on earth, of health and wholeness and pleasure and peace. A time of reward.[40]

Belief in the afterlife and specifically in heaven to come, where we will experience eternal rest forever in the presence of God, is a bedrock belief that can help us not only to cope with stress on earth more effectively but to rest in God more fully even now. Because He has given us, through Jesus Christ, our Lord and Savior, deep hope and joyful anticipation of rest assured in heaven to come soon! This is the security eternal that is the topic of the next chapter of this book, which will bring it to a conclusion. It is a fitting conclusion, a final conclusion on rest: eternal rest and perfect peace in heaven!

*Part Three:*

# Eternal
# Rest

# Twelve

# Security Eternal:
# Rest Assured

As we come to the end of this book, we have learned it is possible to enter into God's rest by faith, in full trust and dependence on Him and His promises. God's rest or peace is available now to those of us who believe in Jesus Christ as our Lord and Savior and thus have entered into His rest. We have seen how we can experience God's rest even more fully through the following ways: Shepherd-centeredness, Spirit-filled surrender, solitude and silence (including contemplative prayer), simplicity, Sabbath, sleep, spiritual community, servanthood, and stress management from a biblical perspective.

We realize, however, that we cannot experience His rest completely and perfectly while on earth, this side of the kingdom! His kingdom has come through Jesus Christ, and we can have a foretaste of heaven as we live in the realm of His rulership. But His kingdom is also not yet—not fully consummated—and hence we wait and groan and long for the day when we shall see Him face to face and enjoy heaven forever and His eternal rest fully, completely, and perfectly! Meanwhile, here on earth, we can still experience God's peace in a restless world; we can still enter more and more deeply into His rest, but not completely and not yet forever. We will still have to deal with stress, trials, tribulations, and difficulties, and the ever present and real danger of overstress. We have to face suffering, illness, and eventually death. But we can do so, with grace and strength from the Lord Himself so that we can experience His victory and His rest and peace in great measure.

We get so easily caught up in the hurried and harried lifestyle of American society today—living on overload or torque—that we do not usually experience His peace in great measure. What would help us tremendously in entering and staying in God's rest more deeply is to focus on our eternal destiny more often: heaven to come. As we have already noted in the previous chapter, people with a bedrock belief in heaven and a certain hope in eternal life and rest to come can cope much better with the pain and difficulties of life now. Knowing that complete and eternal rest in Him is just around the corner in heaven can really help us to stay centered in Him.

### Hope

Lewis Smedes recently wrote in *Standing on the Promises* that "there is nothing more important in this whole world than keeping hope alive in the human spirit…. There is nothing, repeat nothing, more critical for any one of us, young or old or anywhere in between, than the vitality of our hope."[1] He goes on to define hope thus: "Hope is a gift waiting for all who have—a powerful wish for life to be better than it is, the imagination to look beyond the bad that is to the good that can be, the faith to believe that the good they imagine and wish for is possible."[2] In his insightful book, Smedes provides helpful suggestions for developing hope-building habits, discerning false hope from true hope, trusting God to strengthen us in difficult and hard times, experiencing God's power through hope, letting God transform our hope into faith, and looking beyond present difficult circumstances to an eternity with God.

Smedes points out that Karl Barth, the greatest theologian of this century, used just one word to describe salvation: *fulfillment*. Smedes writes, "This, it seems to me, is what our hearts are most deeply restless for—our deepest desire, never totally experienced in this life—the total fulfillment of our very beings that is possible only in God. When we want this, heaven is what we want."[3] Concerning our sure and certain hope of eternal life to come, Smedes concludes, "What this all comes down to is that our 'sure and certain' hope of eternal life is a special, personal, and unprovable kind of certainty that we call trust. We know it will happen because we trust someone to make it happen. We stand on the promises."[4] His own hope regarding eternal life for the children of God is not the disembodied life of heaven but rather an embodied life on earth when it is fully transformed by God into His own good earth.

Smedes' emphasis on how central and essential hope is to the human spirit is definitely right on target. In this chapter, I want to focus particularly on our hope, as Christians, our sure and certain hope in eternal life, and more specifically in heaven to come, standing firmly and fully on the promises of God given to us in Scripture.

## Heaven

Robert Jeffress in *The Road Most Traveled,* about learning to live an "ordinary life" with deep contentment, wrote, "Yet throughout the Bible God reminds us that our residence here is only temporary. Our citizenship is not on earth, but in heaven. One way God keeps us from getting too attached to this life is by allowing us to experience an ordinary life so that we might hunger for something better."[5] Not necessarily something better on earth, but something better in the hereafter, in heaven to come. He concludes, "The unhappiness, unrest, and unfulfilled dreams we all experience from time to time remind us that we are not home yet. There is one more stop to anticipate along the 'road most travelled.'"[6] In stating that there is actually something better, he quotes Philip Yancey:

> The Bible never belittles human disappointment, but it does add one key word: temporary. What we feel now, we will not always feel. Our disappointment is itself a sign, an aching, a hunger for something better. And faith is, in the end, a kind of homesickness—for a home we have never visited but have never once stopped longing for.[7]

In the context of present suffering and possible disappointment, including disappointment with God, Yancey provides the following answer:

> In any discussion of disappointment with God, heaven is the last word, the most important word of all. Only heaven will finally solve the problem of God's hiddenness. For the first time ever, human beings will be able to look upon God face

to face. In the midst of his agony, Job somehow came up with faith to believe that "in my flesh I will see God; I myself will see him with my own eyes!" That prophecy will come true not just for Job but for all of us.[8]

Over two decades ago, Judson Cornwall stated, "It has been many years since I have heard a Christian testify to homesickness for heaven, and even longer since I have heard a sermon extolling the joys of heaven."[9] We have often heard it said, "Don't be so heavenly minded that you are of no earthly good!" We have been accused as Christians for believing in "pie-in-the-sky" stuff like heaven and eternal life in the hereafter, and being out of touch with the real world here and now. So for years we have been afraid of talking about our longings for heaven or preaching on heaven. But times have changed! Today, interest and belief in spiritual things such as angels, the afterlife, and even heaven have peaked again!

*Time* magazine had an eight-page cover story about heaven in its March 24, 1997, issue. Stephen Hill noted that for this article,

> *Time* joined with cable news channel CNN to conduct a poll on people's views of the afterlife. In the poll 88 percent of people answered yes to the question, Do you believe you will meet friends and family members in heaven when you die?... A 1994 Gallup poll found that belief in heaven remains strong, with 90 percent of people saying there is such a place. In addition, in a 1996 poll, 80 percent of people understand that they will stand before God on Judgment Day and will be held accountable for their sins.... Of those surveyed, 78 percent said they believed they had an "excellent" or "good" chance of making it to heaven.[10]

Heaven as a bedrock belief is crucial for hope to be vital and alive in our spirits as we carry on our journey of faith on earth. We need to be heavenly minded enough to continue to be of earthly good! Heaven has therefore recently received greater attention as more books have been published on it. Two examples to note are Joni Eareckson Tada's *Heaven: Your Real Home* and Daniel Brown's *Heaven*, focusing on what the Bible reveals about heaven, with answers to your questions.[11] Based on what John saw in his futuristic vision of a new heaven and a new earth in Revelation 21:1-2, Brown writes, "When most people think about heaven, they mistakenly presume that it will be in the sky, but that is because they confuse it with the spiritual dimensions of the existing cosmos, which as we have seen are above the earth. The place called heaven will not be above the new earth, it will be on the new earth."[12] Similarly, Dallas Willard has noted,

> For example, we can be sure that heaven in the sense of our afterlife is just our future in this universe. There is not another universe besides this one. God created the heavens and the earth. That's it. And much of the difficulty in having a believable picture of heaven and hell today comes from the centuries-long tendency to "locate" them in "another reality" outside the created universe. But time is within eternity, not outside it. The created universe is within the kingdom of God, not outside it. And if there is anything we know now about the "physical" universe, it surely is that it would be quite adequate to eternal purposes.[13]

Many sermons have also been preached on heaven in recent years! One particularly powerful one that I personally heard and was deeply blessed by was a sermon given by my good friend and fellow RENOVARE board member William Vaswig, at the RENOVARE International Conference on Spiritual Renewal led by Richard Foster, Dallas Willard, and the REN-OVARE Ministry Team, on July 3, 1999, in Houston, Texas. Vaswig preached on "*... and the Life Everlasting,*" a sermon on heaven. It was an anointed message from the Lord that moved many of us to tears as we listened to Vaswig powerfully expound on "Heaven Is Real...Heaven Is Near ... Heaven Is Sure ... Heaven Is Creative ... Heaven Is Magnificent ... Heaven Doesn't End!" His sermon was particularly touching as he made reference to his late wife, who went home to be with the Lord two and a half years earlier, after struggling with ovarian cancer. Vaswig is no longer embarrassed or ashamed to talk about heaven, think about heaven, or preach about heaven: heaven has become so real and near and dear to him! And so should heaven be to us all.

The apostle Paul emphasized the need to be heavenly minded, to think often about heaven and the glory that shall be revealed in us, in order to better endure the sufferings of this present life, and thus to continue to be of earthly good! In Romans 8:18 we read, "I consider that our present sufferings are not worth comparing with the glory that will be revealed in us." And in 2 Corinthians 4:16-18, Paul says, "Therefore we do not lose heart. Though outwardly we are wasting away, yet inwardly we are being renewed day by day. For our light and momentary troubles are achieving for us an eternal glory that far outweighs them all. So we fix our eyes not on what is seen, but on what is unseen. For what is seen is temporary, but what is unseen is eternal."

The ultimate promise of heaven to come that is particularly

encouraging and hope inspiring, especially to those of us who are suffering or in pain, is found in Revelation 21:4: "He will wipe every tear from their eyes. There will be no more death or mourning or crying or pain, for the old order of things has passed away." Even death itself shall be conquered, and we shall have new perfect or glorified bodies at the resurrection of the dead (1 Cor 15:42-57; Phil 3:20-21). Paul therefore encourages us to stand firm and be faithful in giving ourselves fully to the Lord's work, knowing that our labor in the Lord is not in vain (1 Cor 15:58).

Over three centuries ago, in 1650, Richard Baxter wrote one of the great classics of Christian devotion, entitled *The Saints' Everlasting Rest*. In an abridged version, Baxter concluded his lengthy writing thus:

> The sum is this. As thou makest conscience of praying daily, so do thou of the acting of thy graces in meditation; and more especially in meditating on the joys of heaven. To this end, set apart one hour or half an hour every day, wherein thou mayest lay aside all worldly thoughts; and with all possible seriousness and reverence, as if thou wert going to speak with God himself, or to have a sight of Christ, or of that blessed place; so do thou withdraw thyself into some secret place, and set thyself wholly to the following work.... When thou settest to the work, look upward toward heaven; let thine eye lead thee as near as it can: remember that there is thine Everlasting Rest: study its excellency, study its reality, till thy unbelief be silenced, and thy faith prevail.... In a word, what will not be done one day, do it in the next, till thou have pleaded thy heart from earth to heaven; from conversing below to a walking with God; and till thou canst lay thy heart

to rest, as in the bosom of Christ, in this meditation of thy full and Everlasting Rest.[14]

In simpler and more modern language, Baxter is saying to us, take time daily, at least half an hour, if not one whole hour, to meditate specifically on the joys of heaven, on heaven itself!! Our everlasting rest is there in heaven to come, and meditating with focused attention on the joys of heaven will lift us up in praise and true worship of the Lord and enable us to rest in Him even now on earth! Let us follow the psalmist's charge to us: "Worship the Lord with gladness; come before him with joyful songs.... Enter his gates with thanksgiving and his courts with praise; give thanks to him and praise his name" (Ps 100:2, 4). We enter the Lord's presence and peace with thanksgiving and praise, singing joyful songs. This is true worship of Him with gladness, especially as we meditate on heaven and its joys! We can also worship Him in silent adoration.

We must not only think long and often of heaven to come, but we also need to remember that we are already right now seated with Christ in the heavenly realms, according to Ephesians 2:6: "And God raised us up with Christ and seated us with him in the heavenly realms in Christ Jesus." As Joyce Meyer has said, "When we begin to lose our *peace,* we need to remember our *place.*"[15] To remain or abide in the peace of God, in His rest, we need to remember our *place:* we are now spiritually seated with Christ in the heavenly realms, and in Him we already have victory! When we intercede and pray for others as well as for ourselves, we need to pray from this place in Christ, with His authority and victory. One day soon we shall literally be with Him forever in heaven. This is our sure and certain hope: security eternal and everlasting rest.

### Security Eternal: Everlasting Rest Assured

Those of us who have truly believed in Jesus and received Him personally into our hearts as our own Lord and Savior can have assurance of eternal life and heaven to come forever (Jn 1:12; 1 Jn 5:11-12). The death and resurrection of Jesus Christ for our salvation and forgiveness of sins make it possible for us Christians who *truly* believe and follow Jesus to know security eternal: heaven is sure for us. We have everlasting rest assured!

In *Secure Forever,* Harold Barker presents strong scriptural support for the eternal security of the believer, as well as answers to arguments against eternal security (based on Scriptures such as Hebrews 6:4-8).[16] I am aware that good Christians of different denominations as well as well-trained theologians have different views on this subject of whether a truly saved believer can ever lose his or her salvation. Without going into a long discussion and debate, I believe that the weight of scriptural support leans strongly in the direction of eternal security of the believer: the true believer. This doctrine has also been called "the perseverance of the saints." However, as John Stott has pointed out regarding the steadfastness of God's love for us based on Romans 8:28-39: "Our confidence is not in our love for him, which is frail, fickle and faltering, but in his love for us, which is steadfast, faithful and persevering. The doctrine of 'the perseverance of the saints' needs to be re-named. It is the doctrine of the perseverance of God with the saints."[17] Great is God's faithfulness and His perseverance with the saints or true believers! This, and this alone, is the foundation of eternal security: it is all of His grace and mercy, not our works or merit. It is all of God (Eph 2:8-9)!

Barker provides many Scriptures in support of the eternal

security of the believer, assured of eternal life and heaven to come forever. Here are some examples for you to meditate on and rejoice in:

*1. John 10:27-29:* "My sheep listen to my voice; I know them, and they follow me. I give them eternal life, and they shall never perish; no one can snatch them out of my hand. My Father, who has given them to me, is greater than all; no one can snatch them out of my Father's hand."

*2. Romans 8:29-30:* "For those God foreknew he also predestined to be conformed to the likeness of his Son, that he might be the firstborn among many brothers. And those he predestined, he also called; those he called, he also justified; those he justified, he also glorified."

*3. Romans 8:31-34:* "What, then, shall we say in response to this? If God is for us, who can be against us? He who did not spare his own Son, but gave him up for us all—how will he not also, along with him, graciously give us all things? Who will bring any charge against those whom God has chosen? It is God who justifies. Who is he that condemns? Christ Jesus, who died—more than that, who was raised to life—is at the right hand of God and is also interceding for us."

*4. Romans 8:38-39:* "For I am convinced that neither death nor life, neither angels nor demons, neither the present nor the future, nor any powers, neither height nor depth, nor anything else in all creation, will be able to separate us from the love of God that is in Christ Jesus our Lord."

*5. Philippians 1:6:* "being confident of this, that he who began a good work in you will carry it on to completion until the day of Christ Jesus."

*6. Jude 24:* "To him who is able to keep you from falling and to present you before his glorious presence without fault and with great joy …"

*7. Hebrews 7:24-25:* "But because Jesus lives forever, he has a permanent priesthood. Therefore he is able to save completely those who come to God through him, because he always lives to intercede for them."

*8. 2 Timothy 1:12:* "That is why I am suffering as I am. Yet I am not ashamed, because I know whom I have believed, and am convinced that he is able to guard what I have entrusted to him for that day."

*9. 2 Timothy 4:18:* "The Lord will rescue me from every evil attack and will bring me safely to his heavenly kingdom. To him be glory for ever and ever. Amen."

*10. 1 Corinthians 1:8-9:* "He will keep you strong to the end, so that you will be blameless on the day of our Lord Jesus Christ. God, who has called you into fellowship with his Son Jesus Christ our Lord, is faithful."

*11. Romans 8:1:* "Therefore, there is now no condemnation for those who are in Christ Jesus."

*12. Ephesians 1:13-14:* "And you also were included in Christ when you heard the word of truth, the gospel of your salvation. Having believed, you were marked in him with a seal, the promised Holy Spirit, who is a deposit guaranteeing our inheritance until the redemption of those who are God's possession—to the praise of his glory."

*13. Philippians 3:20-21:* "But our citizenship is in heaven. And we eagerly await a Savior from there, the Lord Jesus Christ, who, by the power that enables him to bring everything under his control, will transform our lowly bodies so that they will be like his glorious body."

*14. John 3:16:* "For God so loved the world that he gave his one and only Son, that whoever believes in him shall not perish but have eternal life."

*15. John 6:37:* "All that the Father gives me will come to me, and whoever comes to me I will never drive away."

*16. John 6:39-40:* "And this is the will of him who sent me, that I shall lose none of all that he has given me, but raise them up at the last day. For my father's will is that everyone who looks to the Son and believes in him shall have eternal life, and I will raise him up at the last day."

*17. 1 John 5:11-13:* "And this is the testimony: God has given us eternal life, and this life is in his Son. He who has the Son has life; he who does not have the Son of God does not have life. I write these things to you who believe in the name of the Son of God so that you may know that you have eternal life."

*18. John 14:1-3:* "Do not let your hearts be troubled. Trust in God; trust also in me. In my Father's house are many rooms; if it were not so, I would have told you. I am going there to prepare a place for you. And if I go and prepare a place for you, I will come back and take you to be with me that you also may be where I am."

All of these great and precious promises of Scripture (2 Pt 1:4) supporting the eternal security of the true believer in Christ or the perseverance of the saints require one crucial condition: that we have *truly* received Christ into our hearts as our own Lord and Savior, and hence that He lives within us. Martyn Lloyd-Jones put it this way:

> We not only believe things about Him, we not only believe on Him, we are to know Him and to experience Him and His eternal wondrous life being lived out in us. It is wrong, it is unscriptural, it is even sinful to stop at anything less than that. He not only died that we might be forgiven; He died in order that He might come and live in us.
>
> Oh, make certain that He dwells in you, for if He does, your heart will not be troubled, neither will it be afraid.[18]

Wayne Grudem therefore warns us that the phrase *eternal security* can be quite misleading if it is inappropriately applied—too easily and incorrectly—to people who have not truly given their lives to Christ but who have made only a superficial decision for Christ or profession of faith. He writes, "In this way people are given false assurance and are being cruelly deceived into thinking they are going to heaven when in fact they are not."[19] There is blessed assurance of eternal security for the *true* believer in

Christ. But we must not allow the truth of eternal security to be misapplied in a diluted version to people who have *not* truly given their lives fully to Christ. Such false assurance is dangerous and cruel. Grudem prefers the term "the perseverance of the saints," and defines it thus: "The perseverance of the saints means that all those who are truly born again will be kept by God's power and will persevere as Christians until the end of their lives, and that only those who persevere until the end have been truly born again."[20]

J.I. Packer, in his classic book *Knowing God,* wrote a chapter on "Sons of God" and our adoption, if we are true believers, into the family of God as His children. He concluded:

Do I, as a Christian, understand myself? Do I know my own real identity? My own real destiny? *I am a child of God. God is my Father; heaven is my home; every day is one day nearer. My Savior is my brother, every Christian is my brother [or sister] too.* Say it over and over to yourself first thing in the morning, last thing at night, as you wait for the bus, any time when your mind is free, and ask that you be enabled to live as one who knows it is all utterly and completely true.[21]

The apostle Paul pulls it all together for us when he writes in Romans 15:13, "May the God of hope fill you with all joy and peace as you trust in him, so that you may overflow with hope by the power of the Holy Spirit." It is ultimately God Himself, the God of hope, who empowers us by the Holy Spirit, to overflow with hope as we experience His deep peace and joy in trusting Him.

Paul further challenges us to have a specific, focused hope in looking forward to the second coming of Christ. He says in

Titus 2:11-13 that the grace of God teaches us to live obedient, godly lives now and turn away from ungodliness and sinful, worldly passions, "while we wait for the blessed hope—the glorious appearing of our great God and Savior, Jesus Christ" (v. 13). Jesus promised that He will come back again to take us home to be with Him (Jn 14:1-3). He says in Revelation 22:20, "Yes, I am coming soon." May our response be, "Amen. Come, Lord Jesus" (v. 20b).

## Living for Eternity:
## Being Heavenly Minded to Be of Earthly Good

Having eternal security, with everlasting rest assured for us in heaven to come, should be powerful motivation not to live carelessly and in sin, but to live fully for eternity, including looking forward to the second coming of Christ. Heaven does not speak only of eternal or everlasting life with the absence of suffering, pain, mourning, or death (Rv 21:4). It is also everlasting life with the presence of God and eternal rewards, in perfect love, joy, and peace, in complete fulfillment and perfect rest in Him: all in the context of true and pure worship of Him! As the Book of Revelation shows so clearly, praise and worship of God will last forever in heaven! We will also continue to serve God and reign with Him (Rv 5:10; 2 Tm 2:12a).

Eternal rewards in heaven, often called "crowns" in Scripture (2 Tm 4:8; Rv 2:10; 1 Pt 5:4), serve as heavenly incentives for obedient earthly living. Such crowns, however, are not for boasting. They are to be laid before the heavenly throne in true worship of the Lord who sits on the throne (Rv 4:10). Our eternal rewards or crowns help us to worship Him! Our works on earth do not earn our salvation or merit heaven for us. Our salvation, including heaven to come, is purely a gift from God by grace.

Our works on earth as Christians, however, do affect the eternal rewards we may or may not receive from the Lord one day. In 1 Corinthians 3:10-15, the apostle Paul clearly challenges us to be careful how we build on the foundation of Jesus Christ: our works (that is, our doctrine or teaching and living) will be exposed on the day of divine judgment, whether they be gold, silver, costly stones that will survive the fire of God's judgment, or wood, hay, or straw that will be burned up. He says, "If what he has built survives, he will receive his reward. If it is burned up, he will suffer loss; he himself will be saved, but only as one escaping through the flames" (vv. 14-15). Being thus heavenly minded will help us to be of earthly good, and to *continue* to be of earthly good!!

David Shibley, in *Heavenly Incentives for Earthly Living,* said he was privileged to have met a few godly giants of the past in their golden years on earth. Despite his brief and few encounters with renowned Christian leaders such as Paul Billheimer, David du Plessis, R.G. Lee, J. Edwin Orr, and Oswald J. Smith, his life was touched deeply by them. The one common trait he noticed they had was that "they all seemed so conscious of heaven, so in touch with another world."[22] Shibley challenges us:

Heaven's signals are often silenced amid today's clamor. But those who mark their world, as Thoreau reminds us, are those who hear and march to a different drummer. To adopt heaven's values is to live for what matters. And what matters are those very few, highly precious things we can take with us into the afterlife.

We will travel light when we finally go home: our baggage will consist only of souls we have brought to Christ and the intimacy with God that we have developed. That's it.

To divest oneself of rusting riches now for timeless treasures then is only prudent. As Jim Elliot said, "That man is no fool who gives up that which he cannot keep to gain that which he cannot lose." You will never regret living these days in light of That Day. And you would sorely regret *not* doing so.[23]

Similarly, Dave Breese has challenged us from 2 Peter 1:3-11 to go on living for eternity:

The material things people have devoted their lives to—the cars, the clothes, the houses, the diamonds, the reputations, the successes—will be gone forever. Only spiritual qualities will continue to have value.... Spiritual success is the one thing in life without which nothing else is of genuine or lasting value. "These things" therefore—faith, virtue, knowledge, self-control, patience, godliness, brotherly kindness, love—must never be viewed as options within the Christian life. They are vital and achievable. They are the keys to a life lived for eternity.[24]

And such spiritual qualities enable us to continue to be of earthly good, to be a real blessing to others, as we live for eternity, being heavenly minded enough. In so doing, with a sure and certain hope of heaven to come and everlasting rest assured, we will be able to experience God's rest even more fully, even while on earth.

In order to develop deeper intimacy with God, since this is

one of the only two things we will be able to bring home to heaven with us (the other being souls we have brought to Christ), according to Shibley, we need to spend much time with Him daily and regularly, as we have already seen in earlier chapters of this book (see "Solitude and Silence"). To experience His peace and rest, in intimacy with Him, requires quiet. However, as Gary Thomas has pointed out, "Young or old, rich or poor, it doesn't matter—the thing we fear most is quiet. Yet inner peace is conceived in the quiet. Without this quiet, we grow restless and unrooted. Our lust for diversion proves our unhappiness."[25]

One of the most dangerous and potentially damaging diversions or distractions of our contemporary world is television watching! Thomas goes on to say:

> Much of our television watching is a quiet, sleepless death in which we kill our souls by letting time race by. We can spend several hours in front of the television, and what have we gained?... Yet time has slipped by, and it will never return again. In essence, we have willingly forfeited a precious slice of the time God has given us on this earth.[26]

A concrete step to take in order to have enough time for intimacy with God, and deep meditation on heaven to come, on a daily basis, is to fast (fully or partially) from watching TV. At the very least, we can cut down drastically the amount of time we spend in front of the tube. At best, we can stop watching it altogether for as long as we may feel God leading us to do so. My church decided to spend the first forty days of the year 2000 in a season of prayer and fasting. People chose how they wanted to fast: some decided to fast from food (for example, giving up one meal a day or one meal a week), whereas some decided to fast from watching TV, for all forty days if possible!

In writing the last two chapters of this book, I decided to fast from watching TV myself. It has helped me enormously to have more focused time for writing, as well as for reading, reflection, and prayer. I am more convinced than ever before that watching TV is a dangerous and potentially damaging activity, especially for our souls and our intimacy with God. It is not just the time that flies by and gets so easily wasted. It is also all the junk and poison we get exposed to when we watch TV: in the sex and violence in many programs, and the advertisements that pamper our fleshly desires and self-centered wants. It is of course not wrong or sinful per se to watch TV: just dangerous and potentially damaging. We need to be really careful what we watch if we choose to watch TV!

A few years ago, in a challenging article entitled "Christmas Unplugged," Bill McKibben wrote:

> Are you worried about a decline in family values, in community spirit? Then you are worried about television…. If you distilled all those thousands of game shows and talk shows and sitcoms and commercials down into a single notion, it would be this: You are the most important thing on the face of the earth. Your immediate desires are all that count. Do It Your Way. This Bud's for You. We are led daily, hourly, into temptation…. That's one reason I am a board member of a group called T.V. Free America, which every year sponsors a turnoff week in schools around the nation…. Again the emphasis will not be on renunciation; it will be on the great pleasure that comes when you turn off the television and rejoin the living world. And on the opportunity to reflect—

to think—in the stillness of the unplugged mind. Solitude and silence and darkness have always been key parts of the religious life, but they have been banished by T.V. We need to reclaim them and ... break the materialist enchantment that now holds us in its thrall ... that makes us long ... for things that will not satisfy us.[27]

A church friend told me recently that the one TV in his home broke down some time ago, and he and his family went without a TV for six months or so. They had a better and more peaceful time at home during this TV-free period!

For some of us, fasting fully or partially from watching TV may not be relevant, because we may hardly watch TV. Our need may be more for fasting, at least partially, from the computer and the Internet, which can be especially overwhelming and dangerous and potentially damaging as well! Developing deeper intimacy with God requires sufficient time and space: it will mean at times appropriate fasting, fully or partially, from the technological gadgets and devices of our day.

## Conclusion

We have come to the end of this book. We have learned that we can enter into God's rest now by faith and trust in Christ. We can experience His peace and rest more deeply in a restless world, through the several ways we have described. But ultimately, perfect peace and everlasting rest can only be experienced in heaven to come. We can be assured, however, of eternal life and everlasting rest because eternal security or the perseverance of the saints (really the perseverance of God with the saints, according to John Stott) is a reality for the true believer.

Before I conclude this chapter and this book on rest, let me share with you two texts from Jeremiah. In Jeremiah 6:16 we read, "This is what the Lord says: 'Stand at the crossroads and look; ask for the ancient paths, ask where the good way is, and walk in it, and you will find rest for your souls.'"

We have considered the ancient paths and ways to experiencing God's rest for our souls. Let us decide, with His help, to walk in the good way of rest by following these ancient paths.

In Jeremiah 30:21b, we read, "'For who is he who will devote himself to be close to me?' declares the Lord." Let us each respond with all of our heart to be the person who will devote himself or herself to be close to the Lord, to pursue intimacy with Him. We need to surrender fully to Him so that He can fully possess us! Possessed by God, and filled with the Holy Spirit (Eph 5:18), we can walk in the good way of His rest more and more deeply.

David Ford has pointed out that we all need in our lives to cope with multiple overwhelmings, both good and bad, in this technologically sophisticated and advanced age, especially with the computer. He concludes that the wisest way to cope is not by trying to avoid being overwhelmed or expecting to be in control of everything, but "to live amidst the overwhelmings in a way that lets one of them be the overwhelming that shapes the others."[28] His answer ultimately is "being overwhelmed by God" and especially worship of God! Being possessed by God!

The psalmist says in Psalm 116:7, "Be at rest once more, O my soul, for the Lord has been good to you." Yes, the Lord has and will always be really good to you in blessing you abundantly, because it is His very nature to be good and generous and gracious and giving! May you experience more and more deeply the grace of His rest and the rest of His grace.

Sandra Wilson wrote the following words that God spoke into her heart when she was listening to God in Scripture. May you be specially blessed by these words as well:

> "Grace to you and peace" are my gifts to you and all my children.
>
> You have been seeking grace (a favored status) from people, believing it will bring peace.
>
> It never does.
>
> Only entering more and more deeply into the reality of my grace will bring the genuine peace of heart you are dying for.
>
> I already died for it.
>
> And I rose so you would know it's true.
>
> And I have the power to make it true for you.
>
> Hear me.
>
> Believe me.
>
> Learn to rest in the peace of my grace.[29]

And from Scripture itself we read, "The eternal God is your refuge, and underneath are the everlasting arms" (Dt 33:27a). "Let the beloved of the Lord rest secure in him, for he shields him all day long, and the one the Lord loves rests between his shoulders" (Dt 33:12). Zephaniah 3:17 says, "The Lord your God is with you, he is mighty to save. He will take great delight in you, he will quiet you with his love, he will rejoice over you with singing." And finally, receive this benediction and blessing: "The God of peace be with you all. Amen" (Rom 15:33).

# Notes

~

## Chapter 1
### Rest and Unrest

1. Archibald D. Hart, *The Anxiety Cure* (Nashville, Tenn.: Word, 1999), v.
2. Richard A. Swenson, *The Overload Syndrome: Learning to Live Within Your Limits* (Colorado Springs, Colo.: NavPress, 1998), 11.
3. Kirk Livingston, "Tackling Torque," *The Life@Work Journal*, July/August 1999, Vol. 2, No. 4, 32.
4. Bill Gates, *Business at the Speed of Thought* (New York: Warner, 1999).
5. James Gleick, *Faster: The Acceleration of Just About Everything* (New York: Pantheon, 1999).
6. Gordon MacDonald, *Ordering Your Private World*, expanded edition (Nashville, Tenn.: Oliver Nelson, 1985), 161-75. See pp. 164 and 175.
7. Thomas Addington and Stephen Graves, "A Biblical Mandate: The Surprising Impact of Rest on Work," *The Life@Work Journal*, July/August 1999, Vol. 2, No. 4, 24.
8. Addington and Graves, 25.
9. Archibald D. Hart, *Adrenaline and Stress*, revised and expanded (Dallas: Word, 1995).
10. John Ortberg, *The Life You've Always Wanted* (Grand Rapids, Mich.: Zondervan, 1997), 82.
11. Ortberg, paraphrased from pp. 81-82.

## Chapter 2
### Rest: Physical, Emotional, Relational, Spiritual

1. Richard A. Swenson, *Margin: Restoring Emotional, Physical, Financial, and Time Reserves to Overloaded Lives* (Colorado Springs, Colo.: NavPress, 1992), 226.
2. Swenson, *Margin*, 228.
3. Swenson, *Margin*, 232.
4. Larry Crabb, *Connecting* (Nashville, Tenn.: Word, 1997), and *The Safest Place on Earth* (Nashville, Tenn.: Word, 1999); Marva J. Dawn, *The Hilarity of Community: Romans 12 and How to Be the Church* (Grand Rapids, Mich.: Eerdmans, 1992); Stanley J. Grenz, *Theology for the*

*Community of God* (Nashville, Tenn.: Broadman & Holman, 1994); and Rod Wilson, *Counseling and Community* (Dallas: Word, 1995).

5. F.B. Meyer, *The Way Into the Holiest: Expositions of the Epistle to the Hebrews* (Fort Washington, Pa.: Christian Literature Crusade, 1982), 57.

6. Louis H. Evans, Jr., *Mastering the New Testament: Hebrews* (Dallas: Word, 1985), 101-2.

## Chapter 3
### *Shepherd-Centeredness*

1. F.B. Meyer, *The Shepherd Psalm* (Chicago: Moody, 1976).

2. Gary Moon, *Homesick for Eden: A Soul's Journey to Joy* (Ann Arbor, Mich.: Servant, 1997).

3. F.B. Meyer, *The Shepherd Psalm*, 29.

4. F.B. Meyer, *The Shepherd Psalm*, 31.

5. F.B. Meyer, *The Shepherd Psalm*, 31-36. Quote is from p. 36.

6. Eugene Peterson, *The Message* (Colorado Springs, Colo.: NavPress, 1993).

7. Donald A. Hagner, *Word Biblical Commentary: Matthew 1–13* (Dallas: Word, 1993), 324.

8. Stephen R. Covey, A. Roger Merrill, and Rebecca R. Merrill, *First Things First* (New York: Simon & Schuster, 1994), 75.

9. Wayne A. Barber, *The Rest of Grace* (Eugene, Ore.: Harvest, 1998), 10-11.

10. Barber, 11.

11. Swenson, *Margin*, 233.

12. A.W. Tozer, *The Pursuit of God* (Harrisburg, Pa.: Christian Publications, 1948), 116.

## Chapter 4
### *Spirit-Filled Surrender*

1. David Daniels, "True Confession: Are you skipping the first step toward intimacy with God?" *Discipleship Journal*, May/June 1997, Issue 99, 67.

2. Michael J. Brown, *Go and Sin No More: A Call to Holiness* (Ventura, Calif.: Regal, 1999), 17.

3. Sergio Scataglini, *The Fire of His Holiness: Prepare Yourself to Enter God's Presence* (Ventura, Calif.: Regal, 1999), 37.

4. Carol Turkington, "Tavris: Beware Pride," *A.P.A. Monitor*, November 1985, Vol. 16, No.11, 30.

5. Richard J. Foster, *The Challenge of the Disciplined Life: Christian Reflections*

*on Money, Sex, & Power* (San Francisco: Harper & Row, 1985).

6. Leslie Williams, *Seduction of the Lesser Gods* (Nashville, Tenn.: Word, 1997), 10-11.

7. Ken Blanchard, Bill Hybels, and Phil Hodges, *Leadership by the Book: Tools to Transform Your Workplace* (New York: William Morrow & Company, 1999), 172.

8. Sue Monk Kidd, *When the Heart Waits: Spiritual Direction for Life's Sacred Questions* (San Francisco: HarperSanFrancisco, 1990), 53.

9. Kidd, 113-14.

10. Siang-Yang Tan and Douglas H. Gregg, *Disciplines of the Holy Spirit* (Grand Rapids, Mich.: Zondervan, 1997), 19.

11. Bill Bright in Michael J. Brown, 11.

12. Bright, 12.

13. Tan and Gregg, 21-24.

14. Tan and Gregg, 26.

15. Andrew Murray, *Absolute Surrender* (Fort Washington, Pa.: Christian Literature Crusade, 1978).

## Chapter 5
### *Solitude and Silence*

1. Henri Nouwen. *Making All Things New* (San Francisco: Harper & Row, 1981), 69.

2. Dallas Willard, *The Spirit of the Disciplines* (San Francisco: Harper & Row, 1988), 160-61.

3. Willard, 10.

4. Tan and Gregg, 41-42.

5. Ester Schaler Buchholz, *The Call of Solitude: Alonetime in a World of Attachment* (New York: Simon & Schuster, 1997).

6. Henri Nouwen, *Out of Solitude* (Notre Dame, Ind.: Ave Maria, 1974), 13-15.

7. Peterson, *The Message.*

8. J.I. Packer, *God's Words* (Grand Rapids, Mich.: Baker, 1988), 94-99.

9. Philip Yancey, *What's So Amazing About Grace?* (Grand Rapids, Mich.: Zondervan, 1997), 70. Also see James Bryan Smith, *Embracing the Love of God: The Path and Promise of Christian Life* (San Francisco: HarperSanFrancisco, 1995).

10. Henri Nouwen, *The Way of the Heart: Desert Spirituality and Contemporary Ministry* (New York: Seabury, 1981), 27-29.

11. Richard J. Foster, *Celebration of Discipline: The Path to Spiritual Growth*, revised and expanded ed. (San Francisco: HarperSanFrancisco, 1988), 102-4.

12. J.I. Packer, *Knowing God* (London: Hodder & Stoughton, 1973), 271.

13. A.W. Tozer, *That Incredible Christian* (Beaverlodge, Alta: Horizon House, 1977), 122, 124.

14. John Piper, *Let the Nations Be Glad!* (Grand Rapids, Mich.: Baker, 1993), 26.

15. Piper, 79, 105.

16. Tan and Gregg, 42-47.

17. Foster, *Celebration of Discipline*, 96-97.

18. Tan and Gregg, 49-51.

19. David Runcorn, *A Center of Quiet: Hearing God When Life Is Noisy* (Downers Grove, Ill.: InterVarsity, 1990), 19-20.

20. Richard J. Foster, "Growing Edges," *RENOVARE Perspective*, 1991, Vol. 1, No. 2, 1, a publication of RENOVARE (an organization committed to spiritual renewal) located at 8 Inverness Drive East, Suite 102, Englewood, CO 80112-5624, Tel.: (303) 792-0152; FAX: (303) 792-0146. This quote has also appeared previously in Siang-Yang Tan, *Managing Chronic Pain* (Downers Grove, Ill.: InterVarsity, 1996), 99-100.

21. Emilie Griffin, *Wilderness Time: A Guide for Spiritual Retreat* (San Francisco: HarperSanFrancisco, 1997).

22. Tricia McCary Rhodes, *The Soul at Rest: A Journey Into Contemplative Prayer* (Minneapolis, Minn.: Bethany House, 1996), 12-13.

23. Jan Johnson, *When the Soul Listens: Finding Rest and Direction in Contemplative Prayer* (Colorado Springs, Colo.: NavPress, 1999).

24. Dallas Willard, *Hearing God: Developing a Conversational Relationship with God* (Downers Grove, Ill.: InterVarsity, 1999).

25. Leanne Payne, *Listening Prayer: Learning to Hear God's Voice and Keep a Prayer Journal* (Grand Rapids, Mich.: Baker, 1994).

26. Richard J. Foster, "Reflections," in *Devotional Classics: Selected Readings for Individuals and Groups*, edited by Richard J. Foster and James Bryan Smith (San Francisco: HarperSanFrancisco, 1993), 99.

### Chapter 6
*Simplicity*

1. Swenson, *Margin*, 201.
2. William D. Watkins, *The Busy Christian's Guide to Experiencing God More* (Ann Arbor, Mich.: Servant, 1997), 85.
3. Tan and Gregg, 175.
4. Tan and Gregg, 175-83.
5. Richard J. Foster, *Freedom of Simplicity* (San Francisco: Harper & Row, 1981).
6. Thomas R. Kelly, *A Testament of Devotion* (New York: Harper & Brothers, 1941), 116, 121, 124.
7. Foster, *Celebration of Discipline*, 88.
8. Elisabeth Elliot, *Keep a Quiet Heart* (Ann Arbor, Mich.: Servant, 1995), 12-13.
9. Jeremiah Burroughs, *The Rare Jewel of Christian Contentment* (Edinburgh: The Banner of Truth Trust, 1964), 19.
10. Burroughs, 227.
11. Kim Thomas, *Simplicity: Finding Peace by Uncluttering Your Life* (Nashville, Tenn.: Broadman & Holman, 1999).
12. H. Norman Wright, *Simplify Your Life and Get More Out of It!* (Wheaton, Ill.: Tyndale, 1998).
13. Philip D. Patterson and Michael W. Herndon, *Right-Sizing Your Life: The Up Side of Slowing Down* (Downers Grove, Ill.: InterVarsity, 1998), 73-77.
14. Tan and Gregg, 184-87.
15. Dallas Willard, *The Divine Conspiracy: Rediscovering Our Hidden Life in God* (San Francisco: HarperSanFrancisco, 1998), 66.
16. John Ortberg, *Love Beyond Reason: Moving God's Love from Your Head to Your Heart* (Grand Rapids, Mich.: Zondervan, 1998), 170-71.
17. For further helpful reading on personality type and spiritual temperament and how they affect our practice and experience of spiritual disciplines, such as prayer and worship, see: Glandion Carney, *Heaven Within These Walls* (Ventura, Calif.: Regal, 1989), chapter 5, "The Personal Touch" (83-99); Charles Keating, *Who We Are Is How We Pray* (Mystic, Conn.: Twenty-Third Publications, 1987); Chester P. Michael and Marie C. Norrisey, *Prayer and Temperament* (Charlottesville, N.C.: Open Door, 1984); and Gary Thomas, *Sacred Pathways: Discover Your Soul's Path to God* (Nashville, Tenn.: Thomas Nelson, 1996).

18. David Yount, *Spiritual Simplicity: Simplify Your Life and Enrich Your Soul* (New York: Simon & Schuster, 1997), 38-53.

19. K.P. Yohannan, *The Road to Reality: Coming Home to Jesus from the Unreal World* (Altamonte Springs, Fla.: Creation House, 1988), 156-59.

## Chapter 7
### *Sabbath*

1. Leonard Felder, *The Ten Challenges* (New York: Harmony, 1997), 82.

2. Felder, 90-104.

3. Laura Schlessinger and Rabbi Stewart Vogel, *The Ten Commandments: The Significance of God's Laws in Everyday Life* (New York: Cliff Street, 1998), 126.

4. Schlessinger and Vogel, 105-6.

5. David Kundtz, *Stopping: How to Be Still When You Have to Keep Going* (New York: MJF, 1998), 14.

6. Kundtz, 53-54.

7. Kundtz, 17.

8. Kundtz, 81.

9. Wayne Muller, *Sabbath: Restoring the Sacred Rhythm of Rest* (New York: Bantam, 1999), 2.

10. Muller, 3.

11. Muller, 32.

12. Muller, 130-31.

13. Muller, 137.

14. Muller, 183.

15. Muller, 26.

16. Paul K. Jewett, *The Lord's Day: A Theological Guide to the Christian Day of Worship* (Grand Rapids, Mich.: Eerdmans, 1971), 21.

17. See Karen Burton Mains, *Making Sunday Special* (Waco, Tex.: Word, 1987), 25.

18. Mains, 20-21.

19. Mains, 28-31.

20. Felder, 103.

21. Jewett, 164-69.

22. Mains, 39-52.

23. Mains, 118.

24. David A. Seamands, *God's Blueprint for Living: New Perspectives on the Ten Commandments* (Wilmore, Ky.: Bristol, 1988), 73.

25. David F. Ford, *The Shape of Living: Spiritual Directions for Everyday Life* (Grand Rapids, Mich.: Baker, 1997), 138.

26. See Marva J. Dawn, *Keeping the Sabbath Wholly: Ceasing, Resting, Embracing, Feasting* (Grand Rapids, Mich.: Eerdmans, 1989).

27. Dawn, *Keeping the Sabbath Wholly,* 49.

28. Abraham Joshua Heschel, *The Sabbath: Its Meaning for Modern Man* (New York: Farrar, Straus, & Giroux, 1951), 14.

29. Dawn, *Keeping the Sabbath Wholly,* 208.

30. Dawn, *Keeping the Sabbath Wholly,* 202.

31. Dawn, *Keeping the Sabbath Wholly,* 200.

32. Richard J. Foster, *Prayer: Finding the Heart's True Home* (San Francisco: HarperSanFrancisco, 1992), 94-95.

33. Foster, *Prayer,* 93.

34. Foster, *Prayer,* 103.

## Chapter 8
### *Sleep*

1. Hart, *Adrenaline and Stress,* 167, 172. Also see Stanley Coren, *Sleep Thieves* (New York: Free Press, 1996); and William C. Dement and Christopher Vaughan, *The Promise of Sleep* (New York: Delacorte, 1999).

2. Swenson, *The Overload Syndrome,* 126.

3. Hart, *The Anxiety Cure,* 193, 199.

4. As quoted by Addington and Graves, 22, 24.

5. Swenson, as quoted by Livingston, 34.

6. Hart, *The Anxiety Cure,* 196-97.

7. Hart, *The Anxiety Cure,* 194, 200-201.

8. Hart, *The Anxiety Cure,* 123.

9. Hart, *The Anxiety Cure,* 199.

10. Hart, *The Anxiety Cure,* 204-6.

11. Hart, *The Anxiety Cure,* 206-8.

12. Swenson, *The Overload Syndrome,* 131.

13. Charles A. Metteer, *Constructing a Spirituality of Sleep and Work: An Exploration of the Major Daily Routines through Scripture, Theology, and Early Egyptian Monasticism.* Unpublished Doctoral Dissertation in Practical Theology, School of Theology, Fuller Theological Seminary, Pasadena, California, March 1999.

14. Metteer, 24.

15. Metteer, 25-29.

16. Metteer, 31-34.

17. Metteer, 38, 47-48.
18. Metteer, 122-32.
19. Paul Meier and Robert Wise, *Windows of the Soul: A Look at Dreams and Their Meanings* (Nashville, Tenn.: Thomas Nelson, 1995).
20. For example, see Patricia H. Berne, Louis M. Savary, and Strephon K. Williams, *Dreams and Spiritual Growth: A Christian Approach to Dreamwork* (Mahwah, N.J.: Paulist, 1984); Morton Kelsey, *God, Dreams and Revelation: A Christian Interpretation of Dreams* (Minneapolis: Augsburg, 1991); John A. Sanford, *Dreams: God's Forgotten Language* (New York: Crossroads, 1987); and Abraham Schmitt, *Before I Awake ... Listening to God in Your Dreams* (Nashville, Tenn.: Abingdon, 1984).
21. Metteer, 120.
22. D.A. Ousley, *The Way of Holiness: Issues.* Part 2. Latimer Studies Series: No. 46 (Oxford: Latimer House, 1994), 20.
23. See Metteer, 102-4.
24. Arnold A. Lazarus and Clifford N. Lazarus, *The 60-Second Shrink: Over 100 Strategies for Staying Sane in a Crazy World* (New York: Barnes & Noble, 1997), 22.
25. Francis MacNutt, *Overcome by the Spirit* (Grand Rapids, Mich.: Chosen, 1990), 15.
26. MacNutt, 73, 172-73. Also see John White, *When the Spirit Comes with Power* (Downers Grove, Ill.: InterVarsity, 1988). For a balanced, biblical perspective on the person and ministry of the Holy Spirit, see J.I. Packer, *Keep in Step with the Spirit* (Grand Rapids, Mich.: Revell, 1984).

## Chapter 9
### *Spiritual Community*

1. M. Robert Mulholland, Jr., *Invitation to a Journey: A Road Map for Spiritual Formation* (Downers Grove, Ill.: InterVarsity, 1993), 12.
2. Mulholland, 143, 158-59.
3. Rod Wilson, xii.
4. Grenz, 30.
5. Grenz, 232-33.
6. Muller, 183.
7. Dawn, *The Hilarity of Community*, xi. (This book has now been retitled, *Truly the Community*).
8. Dawn, *The Hilarity of Community*, 166.
9. Henri Nouwen, *Walk With Jesus: Stations of the Cross* (Maryknoll, New

York: Orbis, 1990), 35.

10. Philip D. Kenneson, *Life on the Vine: Cultivating the Fruit of the Spirit in CHRISTIAN COMMUNITY* (Downers Grove, Ill.: InterVarsity, 1999), 32, 34.

11. Paul Meier, et al., *Filling the Holes in Our Souls: Caring Groups that Build Lasting Relationships* (Chicago: Moody Press, 1992), 6.

12. Meier, et al., 10. For another helpful reference on small group ministries, see Dale Galloway with Kathi Mills, *The Small Group Book: The Practical Guide for Nurturing Christians and Building Churches* (Grand Rapids, Mich.: Revell, 1995). Also see Carl F. George, *Nine Keys to Effective Small Group Leadership* (Mansfield, Pa.: Kingdom, 1997).

13. James Bryan Smith with Lynda Graybeal. *A Spiritual Formation Workbook: Small-Group Resources for Nurturing Christian Growth,* revised and updated edition (San Francisco: HarperSanFrancisco, 1999).

14. Smith with Graybeal, 99.

15. Smith with Graybeal, 100.

16. Smith with Graybeal, 100.

17. Richard J. Foster, *Streams of Living Water: Celebrating the Great Traditions of Christian Faith* (San Francisco: HarperSanFrancisco, 1998).

18. Robert Banks, *Redeeming the Routines: Bringing Theology to Life* (Wheaton, Ill.: Bridgeport, 1993), 100-101, 103. Also see Robert and Julia Banks, *The Church Comes Home* (Peabody, Mass.: Hendrickson, 1998).

19. Klyne Snodgrass, *The NIV Application Commentary—Ephesians* (Grand Rapids, Mich.: Zondervan, 1996), 330.

20. Victoria Moran, *Shelter for the Spirit: How to Make Your Home a Haven in a Hectic World* (New York: HarperCollins, 1997), xv.

21. Ernest Boyer, Jr., *A Way in the World: Family Life as Spiritual Discipline* (San Francisco: Harper & Row, 1984). For more on how to experience and appreciate the presence of God in the everyday routines of life see Brother Lawrence, *The Practice of the Presence of God* (Nashville, Tenn.: Upper Room, 1950); Jean-Pierre de Caussade, *The Sacrament of the Present Moment,* translated by Kitty Muggeridge (San Francisco: Harper & Row, 1982).

22. Tim Kimmel and Darcy Kimmel, *Little House on the Freeway: 301 Ways to Bring Rest to Your Hurried Home* (Sisters, Ore.: Multnomah, 1994).

23. Marshall Shelley, *The Healthy Hectic Home: Raising a Family in the Midst of Ministry* (Dallas: Word, 1988).

24. Crabb, *Connecting,* 170.

25. Crabb, *Connecting,* 171.

26. Crabb, *Connecting*, 189.

27. Crabb, *Connecting*, 188.

28. Crabb, *The Safest Place on Earth*, 182.

29. Crabb, *The Safest Place on Earth*, 41.

30. Crabb, *The Safest Place on Earth*, 181-82.

31. Crabb, *Connecting*, 203-4.

32. Crabb, *The Safest Place on Earth*, 182.

33. Crabb, *The Safest Place on Earth*, 184.

34. Keith R. Anderson and Randy D. Reese, *Spiritual Mentoring: A Guide for Seeking and Giving Direction* (Downers Grove, Ill.: InterVarsity, 1999), 40.

35. Anderson and Reese, 29.

36. Anderson and Reese, 59.

37. J. Robert Clinton and Richard W. Clinton, *The Mentor Handbook: Detailed Guidelines and Helps for Christian Mentors and Mentorees* (Altadena, Calif.: Barnabas, 1991). Also see Paul D. Stanley and J. Robert Clinton, *Connecting: The Mentoring Relationships You Need to Succeed in Life* (Colorado Springs, Colo.: NavPress, 1992); Howard and William Hendricks, *As Iron Sharpens Iron: Building Character in a Mentoring Relationship* (Chicago: Moody Press, 1995); Bobby Biehl, *Mentoring: Confidence in Finding a Mentor and Becoming One* (Nashville, Tenn.: Broadman & Holman, 1997); and *The Life@Work Journal*, September 1998, Vol. 1, No. 4, "The New Face of Mentoring."

38. Editorial, "Make Disciples, Not Just Converts: Evangelism without Discipleship Dispenses Cheap Grace," *Christianity Today*, October 25, 1999, 28-29.

39. Peterson, *The Message*.

## Chapter 10
### *Servanthood*

1. Steve Hayner, "Playing to an Audience of One," *World Vision Today*, Summer 1998, No. 4, Vol. 1, 5-6.

2. Ronald J. Sider, *Living Like Jesus: Eleven Essentials for Growing a Genuine Faith* (Grand Rapids, Mich.: Baker, 1996), 167, 170-73, 179-80.

3. James Houston, *The Transforming Friendship: A Guide to Prayer* (Oxford, England: Lion, 1989).

4. Kenneth C. Haugk, *Christian Caregiving: A Way of Life* (Minneapolis: Augsburg, 1984), 71.

5. Haugk, 73.

6. Steve Sjogren, *Servant Warfare: How Kindness Conquers Spiritual Darkness* (Ann Arbor, Mich.: Servant, 1996), 83.

7. Sjogren, *Servant Warfare,* 82-83.

8. Sjogren, *Servant Warfare,* 14.

9. Sjogren, *Servant Warfare,* 15.

10. Steve Sjogren, *Conspiracy of Kindness* (Ann Arbor, Mich.: Servant, 1993), 22.

11. Foster, *Celebration of Discipline,* 128-29.

12. Foster, *Celebration of Discipline,* 128-29.

13. Foster, *Celebration of Discipline,* 140.

14. Foster, *Celebration of Discipline,* 132.

15. Patrick Morley, *Second Wind for the Second Half* (Grand Rapids, Mich.: Zondervan, 1999). Also see Art Linkletter, *Old Age Is Not for Sissies: Choices for Senior Americans* (New York: Viking, 1988); Emilie Griffin, *Homeward Voyage* (Ann Arbor, Mich.: Servant, 1994); and Kenneth W. Ogden, "Gone Fishing," *Christian Counseling Today,* 1999, Vol. 7, No. 4, 48-51.

16. Gary R. Collins, *Breathless: Transform Your Time-Starved Days into A LIFE WELL LIVED* (Wheaton, Ill.: Tyndale, 1998), 27.

17. Collins, *Breathless,* 256. Also see *The Life@Work Journal,* January/February 2000, Vol. 3., No.1, "The Life We Leave: Is Your Work a Legacy?"

18. Gary L. Thomas, *Seeking the Face of God* (Eugene, Ore.: Harvest, 1994), 178-79.

19. Thomas, *Seeking the Face of God,* 15-18.

20. Thomas, *Seeking the Face of God,* 124, 131.

21. Thomas, *Seeking the Face of God,* 143.

22. Siang-Yang Tan, "Suffering and Worship: 1 Peter 4:1-6, 12-13, 5:10," *Theology, News and Notes,* October 1999, Vol. 46, No.3, 16-18. Quote is from p. 17.

23. Marva J. Dawn, *A Royal Waste of Time: The Splendor of Worshiping God and Being Church for the World* (Grand Rapids, Mich.: Eerdmans, 1999).

24. Willard, *The Spirit of the Disciplines,* 263, 265.

## Chapter 11
### Stress Management: A Biblical Perspective

1. Mark McMinn, *Making the Best of Stress: How Life's Hassles Can Form the Fruit of the Spirit* (Downers Grove, Ill.: InterVarsity, 1996).

2. Donald Meichenbaum, *Stress Inoculation Training* (New York: Pergamon, 1985), ix.

3. Hans Selye, *The Stress of Life,* revised edition (New York: McGraw-Hill, 1976), 1.

4. Selye, 74.

5. Thomas H. Holmes and Richard H. Rahe, "The Social Readjustment Rating Scale," *Journal of Psychosomatic Research,* 1967, Vol. 11, 213-18.

6. See Jeffrey P. Bjorck, "Stress," in David G. Benner and Peter C. Hill, eds., *Baker Encyclopedia of Psychology and Counseling,* second edition (Grand Rapids, Mich.: Baker, 1999), 1170-71.

7. See McMinn, 15-20.

8. Meichenbaum, 3.

9. See Richard S. Lazarus and Susan Folkman, *Stress, Appraisal and Coping* (New York: Springer, 1984).

10. Bjorck, 1170.

11. Archibald D. Hart, *Stress and Your Child* (Dallas: Word, 1992), 14-15.

12. Hart, *The Anxiety Cure,* 137-38.

13. See Hart, *The Anxiety Cure,* 148-49.

14. Hart, *The Anxiety Cure,* 141.

15. Hart, *Adrenaline and Stress,* 77.

16. Robert L. Woolfolk and Frank C. Richardson, *Stress, Sanity, and Survival* (New York: Signet, 1978), 8.

17. In addition to the books written from a Christian perspective already cited, see the following books written from a more secular perspective: Woolfolk and Richardson, (see note 16); Martha Davis, Matthew McKay, and Elizabeth Eshelman, *The Relaxation and Stress Reduction Workbook* (Oakland, Calif.: New Harbinger, 1982); and Edward A. Charlesworth and Ronald G. Nathan, *Stress Management: A Comprehensive Guide to Wellness* (New York: Ballantine, 1984).

18. Gary R. Collins, *You Can Profit from Stress* (Santa Ana, Calif.: Vision House, 1977), 200-201.

19. Hart, *The Anxiety Cure,* 149-52.

20. Hart, *The Anxiety Cure,* 144.

21. William Backus and Marie Chapian, *Telling Yourself the Truth* (Minneapolis: Bethany, 1980). Also see Chris Thurman, *The Lies We Believe* (Nashville: Thomas Nelson, 1989); and David Stoop, *Self-Talk: Key to Personal Growth,* second edition (Grand Rapids, Mich.: Revell, 1996).

22. Archibald D. Hart, *Habits of the Mind: Ten Exercises to Renew Your Thinking* (Dallas: Word, 1996), vii.

23. See Siang-Yang Tan and John Ortberg, Jr., *Understanding Depression*

(Grand Rapids, Mich.: Baker, 1995), and *Coping With Depression* (Grand Rapids, Mich.: Baker, 1995).

24. Tan and Ortberg, *Coping With Depression*, 53-59, 68-82.

25. Tan, *Managing Chronic Pain*, 58-70, 72-75, 96-105.

26. See Charlesworth and Nathan.

27. See David B. Larson and Susan Larson, *The Forgotten Factor in Physical and Mental Health: What Does the Research Show?* (Rockville, Md.: National Institute for Healthcare Research, 1994); David B. Larson, James P. Swyers, and Michael E. McCullough, eds., *Scientific Research on Spirituality and Health: A Consensus Report* (Rockville, Md.: National Institute for Healthcare Research, 1998). Also see: Kenneth W. Caine and Brian P. Kaufman, *Prayer, Faith and Healing* (Emmaus, Pa.: Rodale, 1999); Peter C. Hill and Eric M. Butter, "The Role of Religion in Promoting Physical Health," *Journal of Psychology and Christianity,* 1995, Vol. 14, 141-55; and Harold G. Koenig, *The Healing Power of Faith: Science Explores Medicine's Last Great Frontier* (New York: Simon and Schuster, 1999).

28. Donald Meichenbaum and Deborah Fitzpatrick, "A Constructivist Narrative Perspective on Stress and Coping: Stress Inoculation Applications," in Leo Goldberger and Shlomo Breznitz, eds., *Handbook of Stress,* second edition (New York: Free Press, 1993), 706-23.

29. McMinn, 39-40.

30. McMinn, 36-38.

31. McMinn, 168-70, 172-73.

32. Ray S. Anderson, *Living the Spiritually Balanced Life: Acquiring the Virtues You Admire* (Grand Rapids, Mich.: Baker, 1998), 5.

33. Gary L. Thomas, *The Glorious Pursuit: Embracing the Virtues of Christ* (Colorado Springs, Colo.: NavPress, 1998).

34. Neil Clark Warren, *Finding Contentment: When Momentary Happiness Just Isn't Enough* (Nashville, Tenn.: Thomas Nelson, 1997), 131-45.

35. Vernon Grounds, "Faith to Face Failure, or What's So Great About Success?" *Christianity Today,* December 9, 1977, 12.

36. Grounds, 13.

37. Ayala M. Pines, "Burnout," in Goldberger and Breznitz, 386-412. See p. 386.

38. Pines, 386-87.

39. Archibald D. Hart, "Suggestions: Preventing Burnout and Stress," *Theology, News and Notes,* March 1984, Vol. 31, No. 1, 20.

40. Philip Yancey, *The Jesus I Never Knew* (Grand Rapids, Mich.: Zondervan, 1995), 112-13.

Chapter 12
*Security Eternal: Rest Assured*

1. Lewis Smedes, *Standing on the Promises: Keeping Hope Alive for a Tomorrow We Cannot Control* (Nashville, Tenn.: Thomas Nelson, 1998), ix-x.

2. Smedes, x.

3. Smedes, 154.

4. Smedes, 162.

5. Robert Jeffress, *The Road Most Traveled: Releasing the Power of Contentment in Your Life* (Nashville, Tenn.: Broadman & Holman, 1996), 175.

6. Jeffress, 176.

7. Philip Yancey, *Disappointment With God* (Grand Rapids, Mich.: Zondervan, 1988), 245-46.

8. Yancey, *Disappointment With God,* 244.

9. Judson Cornwall, *Heaven* (Van Nuys, Calif.: Bible Voice, 1978), 25.

10. Stephen Hill, *Knockin' at Heaven's Door* (Ventura, Calif.: Regal, 1999), 18-19.

11. See Joni Eareckson Tada, *Heaven: Your Real Home* (Grand Rapids, Mich.: Zondervan, 1995), and Daniel A. Brown, *Heaven* (Ventura, Calif.: Regal, 1999).

12. Daniel A. Brown, 190.

13. Willard, *The Divine Conspiracy,* 392.

14. Richard Baxter, *The Saints' Everlasting Rest,* abridged with an introduction by John T. Wilkinson (London: Epworth Press, 1962), 179-80.

15. Joyce Meyer, *Be Anxious for Nothing: The Art of Casting Your Cares and Resting in God* (Tulsa, Okla.: Harrison House, 1998), 87.

16. Harold Barker, *Secure Forever* (Neptune, N.J.: Liozeaux Brothers, 1974). For a more theologically technical work, see Judith M. Gundry Volf, *Paul and Perseverance: Staying In and Falling Away* (Louisville, Ky.: Westminster/John Knox, 1990).

17. John Stott, *Romans: God's Good News for the World* (Downers Grove, Ill.: InterVarsity, 1994), 259-60.

18. Martyn Lloyd-Jones, *Be Still My Soul: Resting in the Greatness of God and His Love for You* (Ann Arbor, Mich.: Servant, 1995), 168.

19. Wayne Grudem, *Systematic Theology: An Introduction to Biblical Doctrine* (Grand Rapids, Mich.: Zondervan, 1994), 806.

20. Grudem, 788.

21. J.I. Packer, *Knowing God*, 256.
22. David Shibley, *Heavenly Incentives for Earthly Living* (Old Tappan, N.J.: Chosen, 1988), 159.
23. Shibley, 160.
24. Dave Breese, *Living for Eternity: Eight Imperatives from Second Peter* (Chicago: Moody Press, 1988), 142-43. Also see Paul Billheimer, *Destined for the Throne* (Fort Washington, Pa.: Christian Literature Crusade, 1975), and *Don't Waste Your Sorrows* (Fort Washington, Pa.: Christian Literature Crusade, 1977).
25. Thomas, *Seeking the Face of God*, 106.
26. Thomas, *Seeking the Face of God*, 107.
27. Bill McKibben, "Christmas Unplugged," *Christianity Today*, December 9, 1996, 22-23.
28. Ford, 24.
29. Sandra D. Wilson, *Into Abba's Arms: Finding the Acceptance You've Always Wanted* (Wheaton, Ill.: Tyndale, 1998), 36-37.